Acknowledgements

I thank God for the eagle-eye editing of Rev. Russ Bixler, Val Cindric, LaVerne Kirkwood, Beverly Miles, and Virginia Steppling, the artistic talents of Tony Condello and Phil Smouse, and the encouragement of Rev. Michael Chance.

I also thank God for Rev. Mark and Esther Butler, Rev. John Custer, Rev. Jim and Monica Flynn, Rev. Mich and Renee´ Kealy, Dick and Frankie Bonifield, Tim Conroy, Rev. Ray Patterson, Rev. Jim and Monica Flynn, Nancy Fulton, Gerry and Janice Frey, Brian and Linda Goff, Glenn and Audrey Harvey, Jack and Janet Hayward, Gary and Fran Kastner, George and Ann Kemp, Clyde Kirkwood, Herb and LaVerne Kirkwood, Betty Koch, Ruth Kohl, Steve and Karen Kowalke, Rev. Bill Logsdon, Bee Marton, Russ and Sharon Michael, Rev. Gary and Karen Mitrik, Fred and Diane Moder, Rev. Mark and Stephanie Moder, Rev. David and Sheryl Morgan, Craig and Peggy Morrow, Ed and Diane Mooney, Charlie and Carol Nomides, Rev. Bob and Nancy Palmer, Jack and Judy Parrish, Rev. Bob and Cathy Pascoe, Rev. J.E. and Betty Smith, Elizabeth Smith, Rev. Cliff and Lindal Reynolds, Kurt and Virginia Steppling, Wayne and Addie Stidham, Rev. Tim and Jill Tracy, Ken and Debbie Welesko, and Paul and Judy Williams. All of these wonderful people deserve some of the credit for the book you are holding in your hands.

Most of all, I thank God for His Holy Spirit, who guides us into the truth (Jn. 16:13).

Acknowledgements

CHRIST'S INCREDIBLE CROSS

Coming Back to the Core of Christianity

DAVID KIRKWOOD

ETHNOS PRESS
The Whole World Needs to Know

Pittsburgh, Pennsylvania

__Dedication__

To every present and future "Soldier of the Cross"

Table of Contents

First Words

Recently a friend of mine innocently asked the pastor of a growing church if he ever preached about the cross of Christ. The pastor replied that he *never* preached about the cross; to him the subject seemed "too negative."

His remark stunned my friend. Especially when he considered that this man was not pastoring an "enlightened" liberal congregation nor a dead church embalmed in the rotting wraps of orthodoxy. This man was pastoring a young church that prided itself on being "evangelical" and "charismatic." His church was full of "born-again" Christians.

How could this be? I wondered. How could someone preach from the Bible and yet miss the central theme of Scripture?

How could a trained minister preach from the Old Testament and overlook the fact that so much of its law, history, and prophecy all point to an event that would take place on the cross of Calvary?

How could a pastor preach from the four gospels and miss their most obvious theme—the subject that dominates more chapters than any other? How could he fail to notice that Jesus viewed His death as the most important event of His ministry, in fact, the reason for His incarnation?

Prior to His imminent death, Jesus Himself had said, "Now My soul has become troubled; and what shall I say, 'Father, save Me

9

from this hour?' *But for this purpose I came to this hour"* (Jn. 12:27; italics mine).

How could a minister of the gospel preach from the Pauline epistles and overlook statements such as, "For I determined to know nothing among you except Jesus Christ, and Him crucified" and "may it never be that I should boast, except in the cross of our Lord Jesus Christ" (1 Cor. 2:2; Gal. 6:14a)?

How could a Christian leader think the subject of the cross is too negative a topic to mention in his church, when it was on the cross that our salvation was purchased and Satan's power over us was broken (Heb. 2:14)?

I sincerely hope that particular pastor is one of a kind. Yet, I'm concerned that he is an immoderate representative of many contemporary Christians, preachers and lay people alike, who fail to place Jesus' cross where it should be—at the center of their faith and practice. Too often the contemporary gospel message is either proclaimed from the pulpit or shared with a neighbor without mention of the cross. Our audience is simply invited to "accept Christ," the One who will give them peace of mind and a more fulfilling life.

But that is not the gospel of the Bible. If we haven't spoken of the cross, we haven't communicated the gospel. *Without the cross there is no gospel.* Paul stated that the gospel is "the word of the cross" (1 Cor. 1:17-18).

Of course, we can only expect biblical results if we proclaim a biblical gospel—a gospel in which the cross of Christ is central. Without a true gospel, there will be no true revivals or great awakenings. As long as the "word of the cross" is neglected, the church is akin to a hamster running on its wheel—very busy but making no real progress.

The Authentic Gospel

As Paul stated in his letter to the Romans, the authentic gospel is *"the power of God* for salvation" (Rom. 1:16; italics mine). No doubt the primary reason for a powerless church is due to the fact that the true gospel, "the power of God," is not being proclaimed as it should. When people are being "born again" by means of a message that does not mention the cross of Christ, is it any wonder that those kind of converts are indistinguishable from those who have not "accepted Christ"?

The only remedy, then, is a re-examination of the necessity, significance, and centrality of the cross of Christ. When the cross once more regains its rightful place at the center of the gospel and our teaching, then the power of God will be manifested unto salvation.

In this study, we will survey an event preordained before the foundation of the world and predicted for centuries before it occurred: the culminating focus of all human history, the wondrous episode that revealed God's righteousness and His love as nothing before or after, the moment when our redemption was accomplished, and the time when Satan's power was crushed. Together we'll probe the preeminent theme of Scripture, the hope of the entire world, the gospel of God—*the incredible cross of Jesus Christ.*

David S. Kirkwood
January 28, 1992

ONE

The Cross
Preordained

In eternity past, God dreamed a dream. He desired to have a family. He wanted children upon whom He could shower His great love. They, in turn, would reciprocate by loving Him and loving each other. Together, they would live in a perfect world, in a perfect society, enjoying one another forever. So God devised a plan to fulfill His desire.

First, God planned to create the heavens and the earth. Even then, He knew that, further in the future, He would create a *new* earth, but the first earth would be a good place for His plan to develop.

Next He planned to create a man and a woman in His own image. They would parent the human race, His own potential children.

The Necessity of Free Will

Because God wanted children who could love Him, He planned that all members of the human race would be given free wills, possessing the capacity to obey or disobey Him. Without the will to choose, they would be robots, and a robot programmed to "love and obey" really *can't* "love and obey" because he has no ability to do otherwise. *Love* and *obedience* are meaningless concepts when no choice is given.

Because they would be free moral agents, the human race would not only have the capacity to love and obey God, but also an equal capacity to hate and disobey Him. Their free wills could result in submission and harmony or rebellion and utter chaos.

God also planned that all members of the human race would be placed in an environment where they would be given the *opportunity* to exercise their right to choose. If God placed them in a world where nothing would be forbidden, a world where they would be ignorant of His will, then, again, love and obedience would be meaningless concepts. Therefore, all free moral agents would have to be tested, for a period of time, to see whether they would chose to obey or disobey.

The first test came in the Garden of Eden. God planned that the *first* humans would be tested by forbidding them to eat from one specific tree He would plant in the Garden.

He would test the other humans in a similar manner, also giving them opportunities to obey or disobey. God planned to write a moral code of ethics on their hearts, and their conscience would tell them what was right or wrong. Then they would have to choose. Later God would reveal His specific commands to test the obedience of those who knew His laws.

God Plans to Reveal His Love

The amazing thing, however, is that as God was forming His plan, He knew that every member of the human race would choose to *disobey*. As Isaiah would later declare by the Holy Spirit, "All of us like sheep have gone astray, each of us has turned to his own way" (Is. 53:6a).

Yet, in the great wisdom of God, this sad outcome would not bring His plan crashing down in pieces. Rather, it would provide an opportunity for God to reveal His great love for the creatures He would create in His image. The Apostle Paul wrote,

> For *God has shut up all in disobedience that He might show mercy to all.* Oh, the depth of the riches both of the wisdom

14

and knowledge of God! How unsearchable are His judgments and . . . His ways! (Rom. 11:32-33; italics mine).

Once humankind transgressed, they would be faced with the consequences of their rebellion—namely, God's holy wrath. Then God would have an avenue opened to prove His love for them. Then He could offer them mercy—but mercy that could only be obtained by His own suffering. He Himself would satisfy the demands of His own holiness, bearing the punishment they deserved.

Even before God created the heavens and the earth, He planned to become a man, live sinlessly under every temptation for thirty-three years, and then take upon Himself the guilt of the entire human race, suffering in their place as a sinless substitute. In so doing, without compromising His righteousness, God would open the door for them to be forgiven. By His selfless sacrifice, the Creator would provide an entrance into His future perfect world where they would live as His children, enjoying His love forever. All He would require of them is that they repent and believe that He died for their sins.

All of this God planned before the foundation of the world.

God's Ancient Book

But there is still more that occurred before the earth was created. God, as theologians like to say, is omniscient, meaning "all-knowing." He even knows every future event.

God knew even *before the creation* which free moral agents would chose to repent and believe that He died for their sins. Accordingly, the Bible tells us He wrote down their names "from the foundation of the world" in a book, called "the book of life of the Lamb who has been slain" (Rev. 13:8). Furthermore, He prepared a kingdom for them, anticipating the time when all the testing in the realm of time would be complete. Then God would have a family who, with pure hearts, would reciprocate His love, a people who could enjoy Him for eternity in a perfect world and society. Then His desire would be fulfilled.

Here is a staggering fact: God planned for Jesus to die on the cross for our sins *before* He created any of us. Only through that self-giving sacrifice could He fulfill His eternal purpose. Such information evokes in us new inspiration and appreciation for God's amazing love.

You can see that if what I've written is true, then Jesus' death on the cross claims unparalleled preeminence above any and every other episode of human history. Words are simply not adequate to describe the momentousness of that preordained event.

The Truth About Predestination

Let's examine the scriptural evidence verifying the truthfulness of this preordained drama of redemption. As we look into God's Word, we will study some scriptures that include an unusual and awesome word: *predestination.*

Unfortunately, the subject of predestination has confused and upset many Christians because of incorrect teaching on this important biblical subject. Yet I ask you to put aside your apprehensions. Once we conclude this chapter, you'll view the concept of predestination in a different light. Any fear or confusion will be replaced with a joy and peace that emanates from understanding the truth.

At one time in my spiritual life I was confused about what the Bible says concerning predestination. I was attending a Bible study taught by a young man who was taking classes at a Calvinistic seminary. You may know that the historic reformer, John Calvin, taught that God has predestined some people to be saved and some people to be damned. And that is what this particular seminary student was teaching me.

Naturally, I became quite concerned as to whether I was one of the ones whom God had predestined to be saved. And of course, Satan capitalized on my ignorance of the Bible and began telling me I was predestined to be *damned.* So I asked my teacher, "How can I know if I'm predestined to be saved?"

He couldn't give me an assuring answer (and neither can any other consistent Calvinist). He only suggested that I examine my life to see if I was living as a Christian should. That gave me even more anxiety, because, like every other Christian, I was well aware of my own shortcomings and faults!

But I soon became suspicious of his doctrine for two reasons. First, it was robbing me of my assurance of salvation, which the

16

Bible promises us. The Apostle John wrote, "These things I have written to you who believe in the name of the Son of God, in order that you may *know* that you have eternal life" (1 Jn. 5:13; italics mine).

Second, I realized that I was being encouraged to trust my *works* for my salvation rather than Jesus' sacrificial death on the cross.

So I began to study for myself what the Bible has to say about predestination.

Calvinism's Fatal Flaws

I soon discovered that Jesus died for the sins of *everyone*, not just a chosen few. He even died for the sins of people who will spend eternity in hell.

John plainly wrote, "He Himself [Jesus] is the propitiation for our sins; and not for ours only, but also for those of the whole world" (1 Jn. 2:2). This one verse clearly refutes the Calvinistic idea of a "limited atonement," that is, that Jesus only died for the people whom God supposedly predestined to be saved. God's Word tells us that God wants *everyone* to be saved (see 1 Tim. 2:3-4; 2 Pet. 3:9).

Second, it occurred to me that if God had predestined some people to be saved and others to be damned, then no person could be saved *by faith*, as the Bible teaches we are.

The only way to have faith for salvation is to know that it is God's will for you to be saved. "Faith comes from hearing, and hearing by the word of Christ" (Rom. 10:17). That is why we are commanded to proclaim the gospel to everyone, so that people will believe the good news and be saved. But if we don't know *who* God wills to be saved, then there is no way *anyone* can have faith to be saved.

The gospel of the Calvinist isn't good news at all. He must tell his audience, "God wills that *some* of you be saved, and if you somehow knew you were one of the people God wants to be saved, *then* you *could* believe and be saved! But you have no way of knowing God's will concerning your salvation, so you can't have saving faith!"

Third, I realized that the idea of God predestining some people to be saved and some to be damned completely contradicts the concept of humanity's free moral agency—a truth found from Genesis to Revelation. Joshua couldn't have made it more clear when he proclaimed to Israel, *"Choose for yourselves* today whom you will serve...but as for me and my house, we will serve the Lord" (Josh. 24:15; italics mine).

And fourth, I discovered that *no where* does the Bible teach that God has predestined certain individuals to be damned or that certain individuals are to be saved. Certainly we can find scriptures declaring that God has predestined us—but not to be saved or damned.

The truth is that God has predestined a wonderful plan that centers around Christ, and that plan has ramifications for everyone. By His foreknowledge, God obviously knew who would and who would not choose to believe in Jesus. Consequently, He has predestined many wonderful things for those He foreknew would make the right the choice. That is what the Bible teaches.

God's Foreknowledge

Let's examine two scriptures that prove God's choosing of us was based upon His *foreknowledge* of what we would choose, not upon His *sovereign decree*. Peter wrote:

> Peter, an apostle of Jesus Christ, to those who...are chosen *according to the foreknowledge* of God the Father..." (1 Pet. 1:1-2a; italics mine).

Paul wrote to the Romans this same truth:

> For whom He [God] *foreknew* [us], He also *predestined* to become conformed to the image of His Son...and whom He predestined, these He also called; and whom He called, these He also justified; and whom He justified, these He also glorified (Rom. 8:29-30; italics mine).

Paul wrote that God foreknew us. That is, He knew we would believe in Jesus, and thus He predestined that we would receive certain blessings. Before the creation of the world, God predestined that you would be conformed to the image of Jesus—becoming a son of God—and that you would be justified, having all charges of sin erased. Beyond that, He predestined that you

18

would be called, and He assigned you a specific place and function in the body of Christ. Moreover, He ordained a place for you in His glorious eternal kingdom with a new glorified body to inhabit forever! Now that is exciting!

The first chapter of Paul's letter to the Ephesians is absolutely thrilling when we understand that God predestined certain blessings for the free moral agents whom He foreknew would choose to believe the gospel. In that first chapter, Paul unveiled God's eternal plan, which centers around Christ. He began,

> Blessed be the God and Father of our Lord Jesus Christ, who has blessed us with every spiritual blessing in the heavenly places in Christ, *just as He chose us in Him before the foundation of the world*, that we should be holy and blameless before Him. In love *He predestined us to adoption as sons through Jesus Christ* to Himself... (Eph. 1:3-5; italics mine).

God predestined all those whom He knew would believe in Jesus to be holy and blameless, as we have just read. Paul didn't say God chose us to be saved—he said God chose us "in Christ" to be holy and blameless. We, of course, have become holy and blameless only through Christ's death, which was predestined before the world began.

God also predestined that those who would believe in Jesus would be adopted as sons through Jesus, as the above scripture also states. Again, it is Jesus' death that made it possible for us to become God's sons.

God's Eternal Purpose

Some people think that God's plan was *almost* thwarted when evil men conspired and killed Christ and that God turned the tables by raising Jesus from the dead. No, that is untrue. Before He created the world, God *planned* that Jesus would be crucified at the hands of wicked men. Numerous scriptures verify this fact.

The Apostle Paul wrote to his beloved co-worker, Timothy,

> Join with me in suffering for the gospel according to the power of God, who has saved us, and called us with a holy calling, not according to our works, but according to His

own purpose and grace which was *granted us in Christ Jesus from all eternity*, but now has been revealed by the appearing of our Savior Christ Jesus... (2 Tim. 1:8b-10a; italics mine).

From God's perspective, His grace (undeserved favor) has been granted to us in Christ *from all eternity* because that's when He purposed that Jesus would die for our sins.

Similarly, Paul wrote of God's eternal purpose in the third chapter of his Ephesian letter:

> To me, the very least of all saints, this grace was given, to preach to the Gentiles the unfathomable riches of Christ, and to bring to light what is the administration of *the mystery which for ages has been hidden in God*, who created all things....This was in accordance with the *eternal purpose which He carried out in Christ Jesus our Lord...* (Eph. 3:8-9, 11; italics mine).

Peter, on the Day of Pentecost, declared that Christ's crucifixion was preordained by God:

> Men of Israel, listen to these words: Jesus the Nazarene, a man attested to you by God with miracles and wonders and signs which God performed through Him in your midst, just as you yourselves know—this Man, *delivered up by the predetermined plan and foreknowledge of God*, you nailed to a cross by the hands of godless men and put Him to death (Acts 2:22-23; italics mine).

We read in the fourth chapter of Acts that after Peter and John had been arrested and released by the Sanhedrin, they returned to "their own companions" (Acts 4:23) and joined in united prayer. It's interesting to note that these early disciples committed themselves to the care of the One who had so marvelously predestined the death of Christ. Luke recorded their prayer in the book of Acts:

> "For truly in this city there were gathered together against Thy holy servant Jesus, whom Thou didst anoint, both Herod and Pontius Pilate, along with the Gentiles and the peoples of Israel, *to do whatever Thy hand and Thy purpose predestined to occur*" (Acts 4:27-28; italics mine).

God amazingly predestined to use what men meant for evil for the good of all people. Those who crucified Christ had no idea that they were being used to play a part in the grand, predestined plan of God.

A Kingdom Prepared

Other scriptures confirm the foreordination of Christ's death. While these verses are not as obvious, they nevertheless substantially verify God's predestined plan.

For example, in Christ's foretelling of the judgment of the nations in Matthew 25, the Son of Man is presented as saying to the righteous, "Inherit the kingdom prepared for you from the foundation of the world" (Matt. 25:34). If the kingdom was prepared for righteous people from the foundation of the world, then God must have devised a plan from the foundation of the world to make people righteous. That plan was through Jesus' death.[1]

Notice that Jesus stated the kingdom had been *prepared* from the foundation of the world. He didn't say that the kingdom had only been planned, but *prepared*. When someone says to you, "Dinner is prepared," that means the food is ready to eat! So, according to Jesus, God's kingdom has been ready from the foundation of the world.

To what extent was God's kingdom prepared? The book of Revelation tells about a marvelous city called the New Jerusalem that one day will descend from heaven to earth (see Rev. 3:12; 21:10-27). Several scriptures indicate that the New Jerusalem already exists and was constructed a long time ago (see Gal. 4:26; Heb. 11:10-16, 12:22-23, 13:14). Perhaps it was prepared from the foundation of the world when God began to work His great plan of redemption.

Jesus stated near the time of His crucifixion that His Father's house already had many "dwelling places," so those dwelling places must have been prepared before then. But apparently not

---

[1] Although the individuals at this judgment were judged according to their deeds, they were not saved by their deeds. They were saved by faith in Jesus, their sinless substitute, and their faith was manifested through their acts of love to fellow believers, just as the New Testament plainly teaches. See Matt. 5:40-47; Jas. 2:14-17; 1 Jn. 3:10-18.

21

everything was completely finished in those dwelling places:

"In My Father's house are many dwelling places; if it were not so, I would have told you; for I go to *prepare a place for you.* And if I go and prepare a place for you, I will come again, and receive you to Myself; that where I am, there you may be also" (Jn. 14:2-3; italics mine).

In the book of Revelation, we discover once more that God foreknew those who would choose to believe in Jesus. In fact, the Apostle John stated that their names were "written from the foundation of the world in the book of the life of the Lamb who has been slain" (Rev. 13:8). If there has been such a book since the foundation of the world, then obviously God planned from the foundation of the world that there would be a Lamb who would be slain. That Lamb, of course, was Jesus, slain on the cross for our sins.

Hidden Wisdom

Writing to the Corinthian Christians, the Apostle Paul spoke of a "hidden wisdom," which "God predestined *before the ages* to our glory " (1 Cor. 2:7; italics mine). That predestined wisdom centered around the death of Jesus Christ. Paul made that clear in the very next verse by stating that if the "rulers of this age" had understood that "hidden wisdom," they "would not have crucified the Lord of glory" (1 Cor. 2:8).

It is thought by some that the "rulers of this age" of whom Paul wrote were not earthly rulers but demonic spiritual rulers who influenced wicked men to crucify Christ (see Eph. 6:12). If that is true, then you can understand why they would not have crucified "the Lord of glory" had they understood God's "hidden wisdom." In so doing, they unwittingly helped fulfill God's predestined plan to redeem humanity!

Were you predestined to believe in Jesus? No, that is your own choice. But were you predestined? Yes, if you believe in Jesus. God knew you would make the right choice, and your name has been written in heaven from the foundation of the world. God predestined that you would be a member of His eternal family who will live with Him forever in the perfect world we read of in the final chapters of Revelation. And it has all been made possible because of the preordained sacrificial death of Jesus Christ. Christ's death on the cross makes every blessing—past, present, and future—possible. *Praise God for His amazing love!*

TWO

The Cross Prefigured

As a young Christian attempting to digest the Old Testament, I found myself somewhat disturbed by all of the references in the Pentateuch to animals being slaughtered and offered up to God. The whole idea of killing animals as a part of religious ritual seemed much too unsophisticated for the God I knew. Animal sacrifice appeared crude, even pagan.

I could only assume that in order to relate to the ancient Israelites, God conceded by reluctantly accepting their own long-held pagan ideas. I imagined Him saying, "Well, if you insist on practicing such a crude religion, I'll go along with it. It's better that you offer up your animals to Me rather than to some idol."

Of course, my interpretation was all wrong. God was not acquiescing to their long-held crudities. He, in fact, was the One who instituted the idea of animal sacrifice, first teaching it to Adam and Eve (as we will soon see). They in turn passed the concept on to their descendants, and God later dramatically reinforced the entire practice in the Levitical Law.

In this chapter, we'll prospect the pages of the Old Testament for insights into the significance of animal sacrifices—all of which served to prefigure Jesus' ultimate sacrifice for us on the cross.

Why Animal Sacrifices?

The sacrificial system of the Old Testament can be a bit puzzling if viewed *only* from an Old Testament perspective. It is not until we stumble upon two very significant verses in the New Testament letter to the Hebrews that the final pieces of the puzzle are set in their proper place. There the author informs us that "it is *impossible* for the blood of bulls and goats to take away sins" and "every priest stands daily ministering and offering time after time the same sacrifices, which can *never* take away sins" (Heb. 10:4, 11; italics mine).

If the Old Covenant sacrifices couldn't *take away* sins, we naturally ask, "Why then did God instruct the people of Israel to offer up animal sacrifices for their sins?" There are at least three answers to that question.

First, there was a real efficacy in the animal sacrifices, yet the benefits they provided were limited. Every animal that was sacrificed could provide only a temporary *covering* for sin and could not actually "take away sins."

Second, the animal sacrifices were revelational. Through them, God continually taught His people that He is holy and righteous, and His righteousness demanded that all disobedience be punished. When an Israelite sinned, the only way to escape his rightful punishment was by means of a substitute, transferring his guilt to something that was innocent. By dying in place of the Israelite, that substitute endured the wrath the worshiper deserved, and God could justly pardon him.

This leads us to the third and most important reason for the animal sacrifices: Each sacrifice served to prefigure what Jesus would fully and perfectly accomplish on Calvary's cross. His sacrifice would not just *cover* our sins—His sacrifice would *take away* our sins forever.

Looking back, we can understand that if God is perfectly righteous, then the death of an animal could not *possibly* provide a perfect, eternal atonement for the sins of a human being. An animal dying for a person would be a grossly inadequate payment.

Jesus Himself asserted that a man is of much more value than a sheep (see Matt. 12:12).

There were only two options available to a perfectly righteous God who is the moral Judge of the universe. In order for justice to prevail, either the guilty person must himself be punished or God Himself must become a man and take the punishment humanity deserved. In this way, the sins of mankind could be atoned for by a single sacrifice of infinite value, prefigured by millions of previous animal sacrifices. Thus we see clearly, as the author of Hebrews wrote, that the Law was only "a shadow of the good things to come" (Heb. 10:1). As a shadow, the Law was not the real thing and could "never by the same sacrifices year by year, which they offer continually, make perfect those who draw near" (Heb. 10:1).

The First Blood Sacrifice

God's revelation of animal sacrifice to Adam and Eve is easy to miss. In fact, this pivotal truth could almost go unnoticed in Scripture. When all the evidence is examined, however, its veracity can't be argued against convincingly.

We learn from reading Genesis 3:21 that after God pronounced His sentence upon the two transgressors, He then "made garments of skin for Adam and his wife, and clothed them."

Knowing what the rest of the Old Testament teaches, we can safely assume God was demonstrating that their guilt could be covered by means of the killing of an animal. He could have just as easily woven a satin tuxedo and silk gown for them, but He chose to clothe them with animal skins. Surely it was an object lesson: A substitute died so they could live.

Looking back, we can understand that the animals that died for Adam and Eve only prefigured the "final sacrifice." That sacrifice would be the One whom God promised would "bruise the serpent's head" when the serpent bruised Him "on the heel" (Gen. 3:15). This prediction pictures Christ's sufferings and triumph. We don't know how much Adam and Eve understood about the eventual saving work of Christ, but it is clear that God taught them *something* about the blood sacrifice.

Further proof for this thesis is found just one chapter later in the book of Genesis. There we find earth's second generation, Cain and Abel, bringing their offerings to the Lord. Abel brought an animal sacrifice, and Cain brought an offering "of the fruit of the ground" (Gen. 4:3). We are told that "the Lord had regard for Abel and for his offering; but for Cain and for his offering He had no regard" (Gen. 4:4-5).

Where did Abel get the idea to bring an animal sacrifice to God, and why was only his offering accepted by God?

The letter to the Hebrews informs us that "by *faith* Abel offered to God a *better sacrifice* than Cain, through which he obtained the testimony that he was righteous, God testifying about his gifts..." (Heb. 11:4; italics mine).

Abel (unlike Cain) *could* bring his offering by faith because he was acting upon God's revealed will,[1] which he must have learned from his parents. Adam and Eve apparently taught their sons the concept of animal sacrifice and passed on whatever revelation they possessed concerning its significance.

In a sense, Cain came with the fruits of his own labor—his "works"—whereas Abel realized that he had no right to approach a holy God unless atonement was made for his sin. Cain came self-righteously; Abel came as a sinner needing pardon. God accepted the sinner who came trusting that the sacrifice covered his sin—as he had been taught by his parents, who had been taught by God.

There are those who surmise (and I tend to agree) that every blood-sacrifice ritual that has been practiced in primitive cultures could be traced to God's original revelation to Adam and Eve. However, in most cases, if not all, the true meaning behind the ritual has become perverted. Rather than serving as an atoning substitute or a representative of the ultimate sacrifice of the cross, the idol worshiper views the sacrifice as a bribe to his god, or that he is "feeding" his god by means of the sacrifice. Those pagan concepts were certainly not what God taught Adam and Eve!

Passing It On

Theoretically, every person after Adam could have been taught about the blood sacrifice by his or her parents. According to the

[1] Faith in God can only exist where God's will is known; see Rom. 10:17.

Genesis genealogy in my Bible, Adam lived to be 930 years old; thus, he personally could have taught his great-great-great-great-great-great-grandson, Lamech, the father of Noah!

To what extent the blood sacrifice was faithfully passed down, we don't know. However, it is reasonable to think that by the time Noah was about 600 years old, he and his sons were the only ones who still practiced it in truth. (And perhaps this is why Noah found favor in the eyes of the Lord, as we know he certainly was not a perfect person; see Gen. 9:20-21.) It's difficult to believe God would have drowned anyone in the Flood who was faithfully offering up animal sacrifices to Him and trusting that his sins were being forgiven.

Clearly, Noah possessed a thorough knowledge of a pre-Levitical sacrificial system. We read in Genesis that God commanded him to take into the ark seven of every "clean" animal and two of every "unclean" animal (see Gen 7:2). The distinction between clean and unclean animals was not in respect to the eating of them, for it was only *after* the Flood that animals were eaten (see Gen. 1:29-30; 9:3). It must have been a distinction made for the purpose of sacrifice.

It is significant that the first thing Noah did upon disembarking from the ark was to offer one of every clean animal and bird to the Lord upon an altar (see Gen. 8:19-20). During the Flood that drowned all of humanity, Noah, no doubt, gained a fresh revelation of humanity's guilt and God's holiness, realizing even more the necessity of a substitutionary sacrifice. (We can easily understand why he didn't offer up any burnt offerings while on his wooden ship!)

Jehovah Jireh

The ritual of blood sacrifice was apparently passed down for at least ten generations after Noah because we find it being practiced by Abram (later named Abraham). Abram could have learned about the blood sacrifice *directly* from his great-great-great-great-great-great-great-great-grandfather, Noah, who didn't die until Abram was about 57 years old!

Regardless of who taught him, there are several references to altars that Abram built as he journeyed at God's instruction from

Haran, through Canaan to Egypt, and then back to Canaan (see Gen. 12:7-8; 13:3-4, 18). Abram recognized that whenever he wanted to "call upon the name of the Lord" he needed to offer a sacrifice to Him first. He related to God through the blood sacrifice.

The concept of representative substitution is elucidated even more during Abraham's testing. God instructed him to journey about fifty miles to the land of Moriah and sacrifice his beloved son Isaac on a certain mountain that He would designate (see Gen. 22:1-4).

As they climbed the appropriate mountain, Isaac, who was unaware of God's full instructions, innocently asked his father, "Behold, the fire and the wood, but where is the lamb for the burnt offering?" (Gen. 22:7).

Clearly, Isaac had been educated to understand the concept of animal sacrifice. Abraham prophetically replied to his son, "God will provide for Himself the lamb for the burnt offering, my son" (Gen. 22:8).

Then, having bound Isaac on the altar, Abraham raised his knife to slay his son until he heard God's voice commanding him to stop. Abraham had passed his test, proving his great love for God. We then read:

> Then Abraham raised his eyes and looked, and behold, behind him a ram caught in the thicket by his horns; and Abraham went and took the ram, and offered him up for a burnt offering *in the place of his son*. And Abraham called the name of that place "The Lord Will Provide" [literally— *Jehovah Jireh*], as it is said to this day, "In the mount of the Lord it will be provided" (Gen. 22:13-14; italics mine).

We read that the ram was sacrificed in Isaac's place. It served as his substitute.

Quite significantly, the place Abraham built his altar ("the land of Moriah") was just a short distance from the spot where Jesus would one day be crucified for the sins of the world.[2] Truly, God has provided for our salvation on "the mount of the Lord" by

[2] See 2 Chron. 3:1. The temple mount in Jerusalem was on Mt. Moriah. Jesus was crucified just outside the gates of Jerusalem.

providing "for Himself the lamb" for the offering.

The words of the contemporary chorus "Jehovah-Jireh" actually speak of God's provision for our salvation through Jesus' substitutionary death on Calvary! It was through His sacrifice that all of our needs are supplied.

In response to Abraham's obedience, God made him a promise. As Abraham and Isaac stood not far from where the Savior would one day spill His blood, God promised Abraham that one of his descendants would bring blessing to *all* the people of the world (see Gen. 22:16-17). He was of course speaking of the Messiah—the One who would bless the people of the earth by providing a way to have their sins forgiven.

Without realizing it, Abraham and Isaac had just foreshadowed the drama of redemption. Just like Abraham, God would willingly give His beloved Son. Like Isaac, Jesus would willingly be the sacrifice. But unlike Abraham, God would follow through—judgment would fall and death would take place. And unlike Isaac, Jesus would actually die.

The Sacrifices of Job, Isaac, and Jacob

Although we don't know the exact date of Job's life, most scholars assume it was during the time of the patriarchs. In the first chapter of the book that bears his name, we are told that Job practiced the blood sacrifice with religious devotion.

It is also clear that Job believed the burnt offerings were effective in obtaining pardon from God. We read of him offering sacrifices for his children for fear they had "sinned and cursed God in their hearts" (Job 1:5).

We also read at the end of Job's story that God's wrath was kindled against Job's three friends because they had not spoken of God "what is right" (Job 42:7). Thus He commanded them to sacrifice seven bulls and seven rams as a burnt offering. Forgiveness could only be obtained through the blood sacrifice.

Isaac remembered well the lessons he learned from his father. After Abraham's death, Isaac built an altar to the Lord in Beersheba and there "he called upon the name of the Lord" (Gen. 26:25). Isaac knew the proper way to approach God was through the blood sacrifice.

31

An incident from the life of Isaac's son Jacob reveals that he, too, understood the significance of blood sacrifice. When Jacob became a changed man with a new name (Israel), he began his relationship with the Lord *by erecting an altar* in Shechem, naming it "El-elohe-Israel," meaning "God, the God of Israel" (Gen. 33:18-20). Jacob obviously knew that a relationship with God began with a blood sacrifice. (See also Gen. 35:1,7).

A New Beginning

Not only did the *man* Israel begin his relationship with God through a blood sacrifice, but the *nation* of Israel also practiced this ritual hundreds of years later.

On the very day of the exodus from Egypt, God instructed the people of Israel to change their calendars (see Ex. 12:2). That day was to be the first day of the first month of the year, signifying Israel's new beginning with Him. Their relationship would commence only by means of a blood sacrifice.

On that day God instituted the Passover, which prefigured, as did every other Old Testament blood-sacrifice, Jesus' sacrificial death for all mankind. In the New Testament, Paul wrote, "For Christ our Passover also has been sacrificed" (1 Cor. 5:7).[3]

On the tenth day of the first month, each Israelite family was to acquire an unblemished one-year-old male lamb or kid (sheep or goat) and keep it until the fourteenth day, when they were to kill it "between the evenings"[4] and mark the doorposts and lintels of their homes with some of its blood. God promised to pass through the land of Egypt that night and kill all the first-born. But whenever He saw the blood-markings, the Lord would "pass over" that house (see Ex. 12:3-13).

There was a death in *every* household in Egypt that night—either the death of a first-born son or a death of an unblemished lamb. It was made very clear to the Israelites that their sons had been spared because the lambs had died. If you attempted to tell the

[3] Compare also Jn. 19:31-36 with Ex. 12:46 and Num. 9:12, clearly marking Jesus as fulfilling the Passover sacrifice.

[4] See Ex. 12:6. It is thought that the expression "between the evenings" means from the time the sun began to set (about three P.M.) until it did actually set, when, by Jewish time-keeping, the next day began.

Israelites that God is not a God of wrath, they would have laughed at you. They were spared the wrath of God because a substitute had died.

Foremost, Jesus' death saves *us* from God's wrath, which we all deserve. The Apostle Paul wrote, "Much more then, having been justified by His blood, *we shall be saved from the wrath of God through Him*" (Rom. 5:9; italics mine).

Notice, too, God's choice of an *unblemished one-year-old* lamb (or kid). It wasn't an old pig or donkey that was to be sacrificed—it was a little innocent-looking lamb, an animal that exemplified purity. Only something innocent could justly serve as a sacrificial substitute for someone guilty. Jesus, the only sinless man, would be the only One who could rightfully serve as our sacrificial substitute.

After sacrificing the lamb or kid and marking their doorposts with its blood, the people of Israel were then instructed to eat it. In a physical sense, they became "one" with the sacrificial substitute. The lamb's flesh became a part of their flesh.

This graphically illustrated the idea of representative substitution. Every Israelite could say that he had indeed received his rightful punishment because what had been killed was now part of him. He was united with the sacrifice.

So, too, as Jesus broke the bread at the Last Supper (which was a Passover meal according to the synoptic gospels [5]) He said, "Take, eat; this is My body." (Matt. 26:26).

We have been united with the Sacrifice. The writer of Hebrews states that "we have become partakers of Christ" (Heb. 3:14). Paul wrote that we are now members of the body of Christ, that we are one spirit with Christ, and that we have been "crucified with Christ" (1 Cor. 12:27; 6:17; Gal. 2:20).

When Jesus died on the cross, every one of us who would believe in Him died on the cross. As theologians like to say, Jesus' suffering was *vicarious*. That means "endured by one person substituting for another."

I like to think about this wonderful truth whenever I hear the old spiritual being sung, "Were You There When They Crucified My

[5] See Matt. 26:17-18; Mk. 14:14-16; Lk. 22:11-15.

33

Lord?" The answer for everyone who has believed in Jesus is *Yes!* We were there, "in Christ."

Our Passover Lamb

The Passover Feast was celebrated annually for fourteen hundred years before its fulfillment arrived in the person of Christ. When Jesus began His ministry, John the Baptist introduced Him as "the Lamb of God who takes away the sin of the world" (Jn. 1:29). This was His purpose for coming, and Jesus knew it. He came to earth as a man to die for the sins of humanity—to fulfill what every Passover lamb for 1,400 years only foreshadowed.

Just before His triumphal entry into Jerusalem Jesus proclaimed:

"The Son of Man will be delivered up to the chief priests and the scribes; and they will condemn Him to death, and will deliver Him up to the Gentiles. And they will mock Him and spit upon Him, and scourge Him, and kill Him, and three days later He will rise again....the Son of Man did not come to be served, but to serve, and *to give His life a ransom for many.*" (Mk. 10:33-34, 45; italics mine).

Most significant is that, according to the gospel of John, Jesus willfully walked to Jerusalem during the Passover Feast (of about A.D. 32) and was crucified *at the very time when thousands of Passover lambs were being slain.* Their blood and His blood were falling upon the earth simultaneously. He died as the Lamb of God, saving the world from its sins.

Is it any wonder that in the book of Revelation, Jesus is referred to twenty-eight times as "the Lamb"? We are told that the inhabitants of heaven sing a new song there, saying, "Worthy is *the Lamb that was slain* to receive power and riches and wisdom and might and honor and glory and blessing" (Rev. 5:12; italics mine).

Obviously those who worship in heaven (unlike many of us on earth) are not preoccupied with the latest theological "winds of doctrine." Their minds are ever fixed on eternity's most significant event, preordained from the foundation of the world and prefigured for centuries in millions of sacrifices: that moment in history when salvation was accomplished, that incredible day when Jesus

34

the Lamb of God died on the cross for the sins of humanity.

God Continues to Make His Point

Our study of the prefigurement of Christ's cross in the Old Testament blood sacrifices, however, is still unfinished. God prepared for this culminating episode of history on a very grand scale. When the Lamb of God shed His blood on Calvary, it would be an event prefigured *millions* of times over and over again.

As if it weren't enough for God to teach the blood sacrifice to Adam and Eve 4,000 years before Calvary's fulfillment and then record its continued practice for at least twenty generations; and as if it weren't enough for God to instruct Abraham to sacrifice his son near the place where Jesus would die; and as if it weren't enough to institute the annual Passover Feast 1,400 years in advance of its fulfillment; God then designed the animal sacrifice to be the hub of the Levitical Law, and thus central to every Israelite's life from cradle to grave.

The blood sacrifice was the only means of gaining or maintaining a relationship with God. The Law provided for daily, weekly, monthly, yearly,[6] and occasional sacrifices, so that one could not live in Israel very long without gaining knowledge of the blood sacrifice.

When reading through all of God's instructions to Israel contained in Exodus, Leviticus, Numbers, and Deuteronomy, one can't help but notice what seems to be a disproportionately large number of verses devoted to the sacrificial system. The lengthy instructions for the construction of the Tabernacle, the priests' vestments and their ordination and duties, the details of the various required sacrifices and their appropriate occasions all provoke the reader to ask, "Why was all this so important to God? Why would He instruct His people to build an expensive Tabernacle and then appoint certain people to dress in elaborate costumes just for the purpose of butchering animals every day?"

The answer is that God was once more impressing upon Israel's minds several of His attributes—primarily His holiness, justice, and love. God was teaching them that if they were to have a

[6] See Num. 28-29.

relationship with Him, it would be through the means of the blood sacrifice.

God was much too holy to have a relationship with sinners. Their sins separated them from God. But by means of a sacrificial substitute God could justifiably forgive their sins, and they could then enjoy His blessings. And of course, the entire Levitical ceremony was representative of what Jesus would one day accomplish once and for all upon the cross.

The Innocent Dying for the Guilty

Five different occasional offerings were prescribed in the first seven chapters of Leviticus—four of which call for the sacrifice of an animal: the burnt offering, peace offering, sin offering, and guilt offering. The four animal offerings differed in respect to the occasion and what was done with the blood and flesh after the sacrifice, but they all followed the same essential ritual. In particular, we will examine the sin offering, which the New Testament definitely teaches was a type of Jesus.[7]

Depending on the person involved, there were slightly different rituals for various sin offerings. The ritual I will describe pertains to a sin offering that was offered for an individual as opposed to that being offered for a priest or for the entire community.

First, the worshiper presented an *unblemished* female goat or lamb at the entrance to the Tabernacle and laid his hands upon its head. At that point, the animal was designated as the worshiper's substitute. No doubt the laying on of hands represented the transfer of guilt from the sinner to the innocent animal.

The substitute was killed, and its blood applied to the horns of the altar of sacrifice. The priests poured out the remaining blood at the base of the altar. Then the fat of the animal was burned on that altar, and the remainder of the animal was eaten by the priests.

This entire ceremony painted a vivid picture of the innocent dying for the guilty, providing a way for a person to be justified before God. Some have wondered if even the burning of the animal's carcass was representative of the torments of hell that the offerer would have suffered without a sacrifice. Regardless, it was

[7] Compare Heb. 13:11-12 and Lev. 4:12, 21. See also Rom. 8:3.

this offering through which God promised, "Thus the priest shall make atonement for him in regard to his sin which he has committed, and he shall be forgiven" (Lev. 4:35). This was the message of the sin-offering ritual.

The Day of Atonement

Of all the sacrifices prescribed by the Levitical Law, the rituals connected with the annual "Day of Atonement," known to us as Yom Kippur, depict the richest imagery. This ceremony unmistakably spoke of humanity's guilt, God's holiness and justice, and the mediating ministry of the blood sacrifice that was effective in covering sins. The New Testament clearly associates the Day of Atonement with Jesus' sacrifice.[8]

In order to understand the rituals performed on the Day of Atonement, we first need to understand something about the Tabernacle where the rituals were performed. Let's take a brief tour of the Tabernacle constructed by Israel according to God's instructions in the wilderness.

From the outside, an observer saw only the curtains of the Tabernacle court, which formed a rectangle with dimensions of about 150 by 75 feet. The single entrance into that court was through an opening on the eastern side.

Upon entering, the first object to meet the eye was the bronze altar of sacrifice. Approximately seven feet square and five feet high, it supported the fire used to burn the sacrifices.

Sitting directly behind the altar of sacrifice was the bronze laver, where the priests washed before offering a sacrifice or ministering in the Holy Place (a part of the Tabernacle proper).

Finally, in the center of the Tabernacle court stood the Tabernacle itself, an elaborately designed tent divided into two compartments. Inside, the Holy Place and the Holy of Holies were partitioned by a thick curtain.

The Holy Place contained the golden lampstand, the table of showbread, and the altar of incense. In the Holy of Holies resided the ark of the covenant: a gold box containing the tablets of the Ten Commandments, Aaron's rod that budded, and a sample of the

[8] Compare Heb. 9:6-12, 24-28 with Lev. 16:11-15.

manna fed to Israel for forty years in the desert. On top of the ark rested the mercy seat, which was overshadowed on both sides by two gold cherubim whose wings were outstretched over the mercy seat.

The priests continually ministered in the Tabernacle court and in the Holy Place as well. Entrance into the Holy of Holies, however, was strictly forbidden because God's actual Presence dwelled there.[9] The high priest alone was permitted to enter the Holy of Holies, and then on only one special day each year—the Day of Atonement.

The Scapegoat

Most of the instructions concerning the Day of Atonement are found in the sixteenth chapter of Leviticus.

On this most solemn day of the year in Israel, the high priest, after extensive preparation and with great caution, entered the Holy of Holies and sprinkled blood on the mercy seat for the sins of Israel.

Having first bathed himself, the high priest gathered the various animals to be used in the ceremonies that day. For himself and his household he selected a young bull for a sin offering and a ram for a burnt offering. Then for the people of Israel, he took two male goats for a sin offering and a ram for a burnt offering. Later, lots were cast for the two goats to determine which would be designated as the sacrificial victim and which would be the "scapegoat."

The high priest first killed the young bull for his and his household's sins. Then, taking its blood, he entered the Holy of Holies. It was required that he also bring with him a firepan full of hot coals from the altar and two handfuls of finely ground sweet incense.

Upon entrance into the Holy of Holies, the priest spread the incense on top of the coals, thus filling the place with a fragrant smoke, "that the cloud of incense may cover the mercy seat that is on the ark of the testimony, lest he die" (Lev. 16:13). Only then could the priest sprinkle the blood of the bull upon and before the mercy seat. Now the priest was considered ceremonially clean and could offer sacrifice for the people.

[9] See Lev. 16:2.

After exiting, the priest sacrificed the first goat as a sin offering for the people of Israel. He then returned into the Holy of Holies and offered the blood of the goat just as he had done for the bull. Exiting once more, he applied some of the blood from both bull and goat to the altar itself. Thus atonement was completed for the holy place, the altar, and the tent of meeting, which apparently had become defiled by those who continually worshiped there.

Next, the "scapegoat" was brought, and the high priest laid his hands on its head in order to "confess over it all the iniquities of the sons of Israel, and all their transgressions in regard to all their sins; he shall lay them on the head of the goat." (Lev. 16:21). This was an obvious transfer of guilt from Israel to the scapegoat.

It is interesting to note that the second goat was not killed like the first, but rather, was led away into the wilderness. Leviticus 16:22 comments: "And the goat shall bear on itself all their iniquities to a solitary land; and he shall release the goat in the wilderness." The Israelites could literally watch their sins being taken away to be lost forever. What a marvelous image!

Finally, the burnt offerings were sacrificed and burned on the altar, followed by the fat of the sin offerings. The remainder of the sin offering was burned outside the camp. God promised at the conclusion of His instruction concerning the Day of Atonement:

> "...for it is on this day that atonement shall be made for you to cleanse you; you shall be clean from all your sins before the Lord" (Lev. 16:30).

Satisfying God's Justice

Clearly, the concepts of God's holiness, justice, love, and the mediating ministry of the blood sacrifice were explicitly revealed in the ritual of the Day of Atonement. Keep in mind that the high priest sprinkled blood on the *mercy seat*, which covered the tablets of the Ten Commandments contained in the ark of the covenant. The blood was brought into the presence of the law of God—the law that Israel repeatedly broke. Forgiveness could only come by means of a substitutionary sin bearer, and the Day of Atonement proved it.

It is with this ritual in mind that the author of the letter to the

Hebrews wrote,

> For Christ did not enter a holy place made with hands, a mere copy of the true one, but into heaven itself, now to appear in the presence of God for us; nor was it that He should offer Himself often, as the high priest enters the holy place year by year with blood not his own. Otherwise, he would have needed to suffer often since the foundation of the world; but now once at the consummation of the ages He has been manifested to put away sin by the sacrifice of Himself....Christ also, having been offered once to bear the sins of many, shall appear a second time for salvation without reference to sin, to those who eagerly await Him. For the Law, since it has only a shadow of the good things to come and not the very form of things, can never by the same sacrifices year by year, which they offer continually, make perfect those who draw near. Otherwise, would they not have ceased to be offered, because the worshippers, having once been cleansed, would no longer have had consciousness of sins? But in those sacrifices there is a reminder of sins year by year. For it is impossible for the blood of bulls and goats to take away sins....By this will we have been sanctified through the offering of the body of Jesus Christ once for all (Heb. 9:24-10:4, 10).

The rituals of the Day of Atonement were fulfilled by Christ, whose work on the cross satisfied God's justice for all time. That's why there is no longer a need for any animal sacrifices.

We have by no means exhausted all that the Bible has to say on the subject of the blood sacrifice, but I think we have looked at sufficient scriptures to impress upon our minds the centrality of this subject in the Old Testament. Just as the author of Hebrews observed: "And according to the Law, one may almost say, all things are cleansed with blood, and *without shedding of blood there is no forgiveness*" (Heb. 9:22; italics mine).

Most importantly, we should recognize every sacrifice offered during the time of the Old Testament served to prefigure the most important landmark of human history, the event foreordained from the foundation of the world—the death of Jesus on the cross.

THREE

The Cross
Predicted

T he gospel-writer Luke reports that soon after Jesus' resurrection, He appeared incognito to two disciples traveling to the village of Emmaus. These two men had been discussing the perplexing events that had transpired over the past few days—how Jesus had been crucified and how some women were now reporting that His tomb was empty. Bewildered by it all, they confessed their confusion to the Man who appeared to be a stranger.

Luke recorded Jesus' enlightening response to their puzzlement:

> "O foolish men and slow to believe in all that the prophets have spoken! Was it not necessary for the Christ to suffer these things and to enter into His glory?" And beginning with Moses and with all the prophets, He explained to them the things concerning Himself in the Scriptures (Lk. 24:25-27).

What a Bible study that must have been!

Jesus pointed out the references to Himself in the writings of

Moses (the first five books of the Old Testament) and in all the books of the prophets, probably including the Psalms.[1]

Notice Jesus expected those two disciples to understand the necessity of His death because of what was written by the prophets. Those two disciples, and others later, finally realized from Jesus' explanation that *the prophets wrote of His sufferings.*

About two months later, the Apostle Peter proclaimed during his second sermon, "But the things which God announced beforehand *by the mouth of all the prophets, that His Christ should suffer,* He has thus fulfilled" (Acts 3:18; italics mine).[2]

Of the specific Old Testament prophecies dealing with the life and earthly ministry of Christ, the majority speak of His suffering on the cross and the events immediately preceding.[3] To be sure, there are specific prophecies that speak of His birth, life, and ministry, but those telling of His passion are far more numerous.

Why were Christ's sufferings highlighted in the Old Testament predictions? Because His death on the cross is the most significant aspect of His work. For the generations who would read the prophets before and after Christ's crucifixion, it was not primarily His birth, childhood, miracles, or teachings that the Holy Spirit desired to spotlight, but the crucifixion itself.

Jesus would one day die for the sins of the world, and God prepared for that event through the many predictions of His prophets. Not only was the cross an event preordained before the foundation of the world and prefigured by hundreds of thousands of animal sacrifices, it was also predicted for centuries before it happened.

[1] Although the Psalms are normally categorized apart from the Prophets, we know without a doubt that David, who authored half of the Psalms, was a prophet (see Acts 2:30). Also, Jesus later said to His apostles, "These are My words which I spoke to you while I was still with you, that all things which are written about Me in the Law of Moses and the Prophets *and the Psalms* must be fulfilled" (Lk. 24:44; italics mine).

[2] See also Paul's statement in Acts 26:22-23 and Peter's in 1 Pet. 1:11.

[3] For proof, I refer the reader to *Evidence That Demands a Verdict,* by Josh McDowell, pp. 181-183. There McDowell categorizes a list of 232 specific predictions concerning Christ, the largest category containing those predictions which revolve around His passion (the sufferings of Christ in the period following the Last Supper and including the Crucifixion).

It is beyond the scope of this book to examine every messianic prophecy in the Old Testament. Because we are concentrating on Christ's cross, we will focus on only a few messianic predictions that foretold His sufferings. In so doing, our appreciation for the significance and centrality of the cross will increase.

Christ's Suffering Predicted in the Psalms

From the cross, Jesus personally directed us to the twenty-second Psalm by quoting its first verse, "My God, my God, why hast Thou forsaken me?" (Matt. 27:46b). Following this "cry of dereliction" (as it is called) the Psalmist describes his persecutors and his predicament, all foretelling Jesus' agony on the cross:

> But I am a worm, and not a man, a reproach of men, and despised by the people. All who see me sneer at me; they separate with the lip, they wag the head, saying, "Commit yourself to the Lord; let Him deliver him; let Him rescue him, because He delights in him" (Ps. 22:6-8).

Matthew wrote that this verse was fulfilled as Jesus was mocked on the cross by His on-lookers (see Matt. 27:43).

The Psalmist continued:

> I am poured out like water, and all my bones are out of joint; my heart is like wax; it is melted within me. My strength is dried up like a potsherd, and my tongue cleaves to my jaws; and Thou dost lay me in the dust of death. For dogs have surrounded me; a band of evildoers has encompassed me; *they pierced my hands and my feet.* I can count all my bones. They look, they stare at me; they divide my garments among them, and for my clothing they cast lots[4] (Ps. 22:14-18; italics mine).

Notice that not only does the persecuted Psalmist, and thus Christ, cry out that God has forsaken him (v. 1), but he also credits God as the One who "dost lay me in the dust of death" (v. 15).

As we have already learned from Peter's Pentecost sermon, there was more to Christ's crucifixion than met the eyes of those who witnessed it. Jesus was nailed to the cross by "the hands of

---

[4] This was fulfilled as recorded in Matt. 27:35.

godless men," yet He was "delivered up by the predetermined plan and foreknowledge of God" (Acts 2:23). He was taking our place and suffering the wrath of God for our sins, fulfilling God's preordained plan.

Two hundred and eighty years ago, Matthew Henry wrote concerning this passage in Psalm 22:

> The sentence of death passed upon Adam was thus expressed: *Unto dust thou shalt return*. And therefore Christ, in his obedience to death, here uses a similar expression: *Thou hast brought me to the dust of the earth.*[5]

Psalm 69 is unarguably another messianic psalm[6] authored by David in a time of distress. In verses 20-21 we read:

> Reproach has broken my heart, and I am so sick. And I looked for sympathy, but there was none, and for comforters, but I found none. They also gave me gall for my food, and for my thirst they gave me vinegar to drink.

This passage was fulfilled when, on the cross, the bystanders offered Jesus "wine to drink mingled with gall" and later gave Him sour wine, as recorded in Matthew 27:34 and 48.

A few verses later, David (and thus Christ) says:

> For they have persecuted him *whom Thou Thyself hast smitten*, and they tell of the pain of those whom *Thou hast wounded* (Ps. 69:26; italics mine).

Once more we see the intent of the cross from God's perspective. Jesus was not only smitten by men but "smitten *of God* and afflicted" (Is. 53:4b). He suffered God's wrath on our behalf.

Although Psalm 88 is not specifically quoted anywhere in the New Testament, which would officially validate it as a messianic Psalm, I (along with others) have always considered it a description of Jesus' anguish on the cross. Some think that Jesus may have been quoting verse 3 of this Psalm, "For my soul has had enough troubles" when He said concerning His imminent crucifixion,

---

[5] Matthew Henry, *The Matthew Henry Commentary*, p. 599.

[6] Psalm 69:9, for example, is quoted in Jn. 2:17 as being fulfilled by Jesus' cleansing of the temple, and Psalm 69:4 is quoted in Jn. 15:25, as being fulfilled by Jesus who "was hated without a cause."

"Now My soul has become troubled...", recorded in John 12:27. Regardless, this psalm is certainly the most melancholy of all the Psalms. For example, we read,

> I am reckoned among those who go down to the pit; I have become like a man without strength, forsaken among the dead, like the slain who lie in the grave, whom Thou dost remember no more, and they are cut off from Thy hand. Thou hast put me in the lowest pit, in dark places, in the depths. *Thy wrath has rested upon me, and Thou hast afflicted me with all Thy waves.* Thou hast removed my acquaintances far from me; Thou hast made me an object of loathing to them; I am shut up and cannot go out....I was afflicted and about to die from my youth on; I suffer Thy terrors; I am overcome. *Thy burning anger has passed over me; Thy terrors have destroyed me. They have surrounded me like water all day long; they have encompassed me altogether* (Ps. 88:4-8, 15-17; italics mine).

It certainly seems reasonable to surmise that this Psalm prophetically speaks of the terrors Christ experienced on the cross for our sakes.

Isaiah's Foretelling

More than any other chapter in the Old Testament, the fifty-third chapter of Isaiah describes the significance of Jesus' work on the cross. Jesus Himself quoted from it just before His arrest and trial, and portions of it are quoted at least four other times in the New Testament.[7]

Just as surely as the third chapter of Romans could be considered the central chapter (from a theological perspective) of the New Testament, the fifty-third chapter of Isaiah can be considered the central chapter of the Old Testament. It is well worth quoting the entire chapter, which I will do, adding commentary as we proceed.

> Who has believed our message? And to whom has the arm of the Lord been revealed? For He [Jesus] grew up before Him [God the Father] like a tender shoot, and like a root out

---

[7] See Matt. 8:17; Luke 22:37; Acts 8:32; 1 Pet. 2:22, 24.

of parched ground; He has no stately form or majesty that we should look upon Him, nor appearance that we should be attracted to Him. He was despised and forsaken of men, a man of sorrows, and acquainted with grief; and like one from whom men hide their face, He was despised, and we did not esteem Him (Is. 53:1-3).

Jesus was despised and forsaken to a certain degree during His entire life, but there was no time when He was virtually universally despised and forsaken other than during His trial and crucifixion.

Surely our griefs [literally "sickness"] He Himself bore, and our sorrows [literally "pains"] He carried; yet we ourselves esteemed Him stricken, smitten of God, and afflicted (Is. 53:4).

Once again we read of God's intent from the beginning being fulfilled on the cross. Jesus suffered not only the hatred of men but also the wrath of God. Isaiah further elaborated on this theme as no other Old Testament writer:

But He was pierced through for our transgressions, He was crushed for our iniquities; the chastening for our well-being [literally "peace"] fell upon Him, and by His scourging we are healed. All of us like sheep have gone astray, each of us has turned to his own way; but the Lord has caused the iniquity of us all to fall on Him (Is. 53:5-6).

That is precisely what occurred on the cross. Jesus bore our sins—our guilt was transferred to Him, and He became liable for our penalty.

Continuing, Isaiah spoke of Jesus' trials, during which He remained silent before His accusers:[8]

He was oppressed and He was afflicted, yet He did not open His mouth; like a lamb that is led to slaughter, and like a sheep that is silent before its shearers, so He did not open His mouth. By oppression and judgment He was taken away; and as for His generation, who considered that He was cut off out of the land of the living, for the transgression of my

[8] See Matt. 26:63; 27:12-14 for the fulfillment.

people to whom the stroke was due? (Is. 53:7-8).

I encourage you to re-read that last sentence. Isaiah was saying that no one of Jesus' generation, as they watched Him die, had any idea He was suffering death because He was taking the punishment due them.

> His grave was assigned to be with wicked men [the two thieves who were crucified with Him], yet with a rich man in His death [Jesus was buried in a rich man's tomb; see Matt. 27:57-60]; although He had done no violence, nor was their any deceit found in His mouth (Is. 53:9).

Jesus was sinless.

> But the Lord was pleased to crush Him, putting Him to grief; if He would render Himself as a guilt offering, He will see His offspring, He will prolong His days, and the good pleasure of the Lord will prosper in His hand (Is. 53:10).

This verse again teaches God's purpose in Christ's death. As we studied in the previous chapter, the Levitical sacrifices typified Jesus' sacrifice, and here Isaiah stated that Jesus became a guilt offering.

This passage also indicates that the One who would be "cut off out of the land of the living" would obviously live again, and He would "see His offspring" (those of us who would believe in Him) and would "prolong His days."

> As a result of the anguish of His soul, He will see it and be satisfied; by His knowledge the Righteous One, My Servant, will justify the many, as He will bear their iniquities (Is. 53:11).

There is the gospel of Jesus Christ in a nutshell. We are justified because He bore our iniquities.

> Therefore, I will allot Him a portion with the great, and He will divide the booty with the strong; Because He poured out Himself to death, and was numbered with the transgressors; yet He Himself bore the sin of many, and interceded for the transgressors (Is. 53:12).

Some commentators see Isaiah's statement that the Messiah

47

would "be numbered with the transgressors" as a reference to Jesus' dying with the two thieves.[9] The statement that He would "intercede for the transgressors" is often considered a reference to His intercession for the thief who requested mercy or possibly His prayer for God to forgive the Roman soldiers who divided His garments.

These, no doubt, are correct interpretations, but those statements have an even better application to what Jesus did for all of us. He took upon Himself *our* sin, and thus was identified with "the transgressors." *We're all transgressors.*

And He "always lives to make intercession" for us as the author of Hebrews wrote (Heb. 7:25). Jesus is everyone's Intercessor, the go-between between man and God.

Now allow me to end this chapter as I began it. Of all the specific predictions found in the Old Testament concerning Christ's birth, life, and earthly ministry, the bulk of them deal with His crucifixion.

Jesus fulfilled more specific Old Testament messianic predictions concerning His life and ministry during His final day on earth than He did during all the rest of His earthly life. Should we not then view Christ's death on the cross just as the Holy Spirit did and does, as the most significant aspect of His earthly ministry? Certainly we should.

[9] A questionable verse found in Mark 15:28 supports this view.

FOUR

The Savior Presented

Thus far we have learned that the death of Christ was preor-dained from the foundation of the world, prefigured by millions of animal sacrifices spanning thousands of years, and predicted by the prophets for centuries. There was no half-hearted preparation for the event that would make it possible for God to justly offer a free and full pardon to billions of sinners!

Finally, God's chosen time out of all eternity arrived—the time for the fulfillment of His eternal plan; the time when God would become a man. The Apostle Paul refers to that very special period of history as "the fulness of the time":

> But when the fulness of the time came, God sent forth His Son, born of a woman, born under the Law, in order that He might redeem those who were under the Law, that we might receive adoption as sons (Gal. 4:4).

The birth of Jesus in Bethlehem of Judea was not the beginning of a new life, as in the case of every other human birth, but was the continuation of an eternal life. The Son of God did not begin His existence in a stable but existed from eternity past. He became a man but was still fully God. As the prophet Isaiah said, "For a child will be born to us, a son will be given to us"(Is. 9:6). The human child was born, but the divine Son was given.

Why Did Jesus Become a Man?

Why did Jesus become a man? The simple answer is that He had to become a human being in order to die for humanity's sins. As the above quoted scripture states, Jesus was "born of a woman." That means He became a human being. His purpose in becoming a man, as Paul stated, was to redeem us. Of course, our redemption was accomplished by His sacrificial death, but unless He had lived as a man, He could not have died as a man.

Jesus was born to die. Certainly Jesus did many wonderful things during His earthly ministry, but those were not the primary reason for His incarnation. As He Himself proclaimed, He came "to give His life a ransom for many" (Mk. 10:45).

The primary purpose of the incarnation was so that the God-man could suffer and die. This truth is contained in other scriptures as well. For example, we read in the book of Hebrews:

> Since then the children [those of us who would believe in Him] share in flesh and blood [we have human bodies], He Himself likewise also partook of the same [a human body], that *through death* He might render powerless him who had the power of death, that is, the devil..."(Heb. 2:14-15; italics mine).

Jesus "partook of flesh and blood" so that He could physically die. And through His death, Satan was rendered powerless. (We'll study Satan's demise in a later chapter.)

His Birth a Revelation

The story of Christ's conception helps us understand the purpose for His incarnation.

We read that an angel appeared in a dream to Joseph and instructed him to name Mary's Child *Jesus,* or the Hebrew *Yehoshua,* which means "Jehovah saves." The angel gave the reason for this name when he explained, "It is He who will save His people from their sins" (Matt. 1:21).

Looking back, we, of course, know that it was only through Jesus' death that we have been saved from our sins. It's easy for us to see the prediction of the death of Christ even in the disclosure of His miraculous conception. The angel didn't say, "Jesus will heal and teach and deliver people from demons." All of those things were significant in themselves, but none compares with the primary purpose of His incarnation—to die for our sins as a man.

On the night of Jesus' birth, an angel also appeared to some shepherds and once again proclaimed the reason for the Messiah's birth:

> For today in the city of David there has been born *for you a Savior,* who is Christ the Lord" (Lk. 2:11; italics mine).

Notice the angel said Jesus had been born *for them.* And notice He had been born for them *a Savior*—the One who would accomplish salvation. Again, we realize that salvation was accomplished through His death. For that reason Jesus became a man.

The Apostles Paul and John respectively add their testimonies to this fact:

> It is a trustworthy statement, deserving full acceptance, that Christ Jesus *came into the world* to save sinners...(1 Tim. 1:15; italics mine).

> And you know that *He appeared* in order to take away sins...(1 Jn. 3:5; italics mine).

According to Scripture, the incarnation was absolutely essential for our salvation. Unless God became a man, there would be no way we could hope to escape the punishment we deserve.

Fully Tested

Not only was it essential that God become a man, but it was also crucial for that God-man to live for an extended period of time on earth. Why? Because He had to be proven sinless in order to qualify as our substitute. The only way He could be declared sinless was to be tempted with the temptations that all other people have faced.

Only one without guilt could justly serve as our substitute, otherwise He would be deserving of the same condemnation as we. If a man on death row volunteered to die in place of his friend who was also on death row, his offer would be unacceptable. Why? Because he himself is under sentence of death for his own offense. *It would take someone who was without sin to redeem us.*

If it had only been necessary for God to become a man and then die, without living a life full of temptation, Jesus could very well have completed His mission by dying with the other babies of Bethlehem who were killed by Herod's cruel decree. But it was necessary for Jesus to be *fully tested* and *proven sinless* before dying.

As we examine Scripture, it seems safe to say that God does not consider a man to have been sufficiently tested until he has reached at least the age of thirty. For example, Joseph, after many trials, was exalted in Egypt at age thirty.[1] David, after years of difficulties, was exalted to kingship at age thirty.[2] The Levites entered their priestly responsibilities at age thirty.[3] Very possibly, Ezekiel began his ministry at age thirty.[4] Jesus entered His ministry at about age thirty after *first* being led by the Holy Spirit into the wilderness to be severely tempted by the devil.[5]

And we must not think that the wilderness temptation was the first and last time Jesus ever faced temptation. Scripture plainly states that after Jesus' temptation episode in the wilderness, the devil "departed from Him until an opportune time" (Lk. 4:13). It is clear that Jesus was further tempted at later times.

Jesus had also been tempted *prior* to His episode with Satan in the wilderness. The writer of Hebrews stated that Jesus was "tempted in all things as we are, yet without sin" (Heb. 4:15b). Jesus was tempted in every way, all through His life, just as we are. We have been tempted as children, as teenagers, and as adults. So was Jesus.

No doubt He was tempted to perform slipshod work in His father's carpenter shop or to cheat a customer in some other way. Jesus was tempted to lie, to lust, to hate, but He never yielded. And in so doing, He proved Himself to be sinless. He demonstrated His qualification to die for mankind as the sinless substitute, which God's righteousness required if anyone was to be saved.

[1] See Gen. 41:46. [2] See 2 Sam. 5:4. [3] See Num. 4:2-3, 22-23, 29-30, 46-47.
[4] See Ezek. 1:1. [5] See Matt. 4:1.

Think about it: If Jesus had yielded to a single temptation during His lifetime it would have meant that none of us could be saved! *Praise God that Jesus never sinned!*

Why Was Jesus Water Baptized?

Finally, after thirty years of living the life of a human being, after thirty years of facing daily temptation, after thirty years of sinless submission to God's will, Jesus entered into His ministry. It seems strange, however, that His first act was to be baptized by John in the Jordan River.

Initially John objected to Jesus' request for baptism, and we can certainly understand his hesitancy. Jesus was the Savior, and John was a sinner who needed a Savior. What right did he have to baptize the Savior?

Moreover, why was the Savior even submitting to baptism, especially since it was considered a "baptism of repentance" for sinners (Lk. 3:3)?

Jesus answered John's objection by stating, "Permit it at this time; for in this way it is fitting for us to fulfill all righteousness" (Matt. 3:15).

If Jesus had nothing of which to repent, why did He insist on being baptized? There can be only one reason: He was identifying Himself with sinners—a foreshadowing of the primary purpose of His coming, which would be fulfilled on the cross when He would bear every person's sins. His death would truly "fulfill all righteousness" by providing the means whereby God could righteously forgive undeserving sinners.

Concerning Christ' baptism, James Denney wrote:

> Here in the baptism we see...*Jesus numbering Himself with the transgressors,* submitting to be baptized with their baptism, identifying Himself with them in their relation to God as sinners, making all their responsibilities His own....It was no accident that now, and not at some other hour, the Father's voice declared Him the beloved Son, the chosen One in whom His soul delighted. For in so identifying Himself with sinful men, in so making their last and most dreadful responsibilities His own, Jesus approved Himself

the true Son of the Father, the true Servant and Representative of Him whose name from of old is Redeemer.[6]

The foreshadowing of the cross at Jesus' baptism is further substantiated by a later statement Jesus made concerning His death, which He metaphorically referred to as a baptism:

"But I have a baptism to undergo, and how distressed I am until it is accomplished!" (Lk. 12:50).

It seems quite reasonable to surmise that Jesus was referring here to His death. This becomes especially clear in light of a later statement in which He used the same metaphor (baptism) as a reference to the sufferings He would shortly endure on the cross (see Mk. 10:36-40).

So we see that not only was the purpose of Christ's incarnation revealed at His conception and birth, but His sacrificial death for sinners was foreshadowed at the inauguration of His ministry. It was then that John the Baptist introduced Him as "the Lamb of God who takes away the sin of the world!" (Jn. 1:29b).

"I Lay Down My Life"

Throughout the three years of His ministry, Jesus made numerous references to His death. In fact, these statements became more frequent as the final day approached. Many of the early references were purposely vague, but nevertheless, are clear to those of us who read them from a post-crucifixion view.

For example, in His discourse with Nicodemus, Jesus predicted both His crucifixion and its accomplishment: "And as Moses lifted up the serpent in the wilderness, even so must the Son of Man be lifted up; that whoever believes in Him may have eternal life" (Jn. 3:14-15).

When the Pharisees complained to Jesus that His disciples never fasted, He replied that the bridegroom's attendants do not fast as long as the bridegroom is with them. Jesus went on to predict that one day the bridegroom would be taken away; then the attendants would fast (see Lk. 5:33-35).

When the scribes and Pharisees requested a sign from Him,

---

[6] James Denney, *The Death of Christ*, p. 15.

Jesus replied that there would be no sign given but the sign of Jonah. What did that mean? He would spend three days and nights in the heart of the earth just as Jonah did in the belly of the fish (see Matt. 12:38-40).

In John 6 we read of Jesus telling His Jewish audience, "I am the living bread that came down out of heaven; if anyone eats of this bread, he shall live forever; and the bread also which I shall give for the life of the world is My flesh" (Jn 6:51).

Later in John's gospel, Jesus proclaimed, "I am the good shepherd; the good shepherd lays down His life for the sheep....For this reason the Father loves Me, because I lay down My life that I may take it again" (Jn. 10:11,17).

These statements alone make it clear that Jesus viewed His death as His most significant work.

Predicting His Own Death

Anyone who surveys the four gospels can't help but notice what seems to be a disproportionately large amount of space devoted to Christ's final days and crucifixion. Of a combined total of eighty-nine chapters, twenty-six concern themselves with the events of Jesus' final week.

Potentially, the gospel writers could have recorded incidents of *any* of the twelve thousand days of Jesus' life, yet they were inspired to devote almost *one-third* of their writings to reporting the final *six or seven days* of His earthly life. Obviously the Holy Spirit wants to draw our attention to Jesus' death.

As the culminating day of history drew closer, Jesus predicted His death much more frequently and plainly than any time previously, underscoring its necessity. It would be no accident that He would die a horrible death. It was God's preordained plan. It was the primary purpose for His coming.

Mark's gospel records eight separate occasions when Jesus predicted His death.[7]

The first, recorded in chapter eight, occurred directly after Peter had made his impressive confession of Jesus' messiahship and divinity. Now that His disciples knew who He was, it was impor-

---

[7] Mk. 8:31-33; 9:12; 9:31; 10:32-34; 10:45; 12:1-8; 14:7-8; 14:22-28

tant that they understand what He came to accomplish.

So after commending Peter and then warning His disciples not to reveal His identity, Jesus "began to teach them that the Son of Man must suffer many things and be rejected by the elders and the chief priests and the scribes, and be killed, and after three days rise again" (Mk. 8:31).

The Scripture goes on to say that "He was stating the matter plainly," with the result that "Peter took Him aside and began to rebuke Him" (Mk. 8:32). That the divine Son of God, the Messiah of Israel, should die was unthinkable to Peter. Surely Jesus had made a misstatement. Peter was so certain that the death of Jesus could not possibly be God's will that he boldly rebuked the Master, first taking Him aside so as not to embarrass Him!

But Jesus' response surely must have shocked Peter. Having been commended just a minute before for his godly understanding of Jesus' identity, now Peter finds himself being rebuked for adopting a humanistic perspective of God's ultimate purpose in sending Christ:

> But turning around and seeing His disciples, He rebuked Peter, and said, *"Get behind Me, Satan; for you are not setting your mind on God's interests, but man's"* (Mk. 8:33; italics mine).

It is clear that Jesus wanted to leave a lasting impression upon Peter and the disciples' minds concerning God's viewpoint of His imminent death: *It was God's intention for Him to die.* Any other perspective was utterly unacceptable.

And why was it God's intention that Jesus die? Because only then could the holy God, the Judge of the universe, justly offer a free pardon to the human beings He loved so much.

"The Hour Has Come..."

John's gospel, although not recording Jesus' *specific* predictions of His death, does include a repeated use of what is first a cryptic phrase, but which later is revealed as an obvious reference to the hour of His crucifixion. I list the first four references below:

> And Jesus said to her, "Woman what do I have to do with you? *My hour has not yet come*" (Jn. 2:4; italics mine).

"Go up to the feast yourselves; I do not go up to this feast because *My time has not yet fully come*" (Jn. 7:8; italics mine).

They were seeking therefore to seize Him; and no man laid his hand on Him, because *His hour had not yet come* (Jn. 7:30; italics mine).

These words He spoke in the treasury, as He taught in the temple; and no one seized him, *because His hour had not yet come* (Jn. 8:20; italics mine).

It becomes clear in the third and fourth references that "the hour" of which John wrote had something to do with Jesus falling into the hands of men. The fifth, sixth, and seventh references listed below all occurred during the final few days of His earthly life, and "the hour" becomes obvious as a reference to His death:

Now before the Feast of the Passover, Jesus knowing that *His hour had come* that He should depart out of this world to the Father... (Jn. 13:1; italics mine).

These things Jesus spoke; and lifting up His eyes to heaven, He said, "Father, *the hour has come;* glorify Thy Son, that the Son may glorify Thee..." (Jn. 17:1: italics mine).

And Jesus answered them, saying, "*The hour has come* for the Son of Man to be glorified. Truly, truly, I say to you, unless a grain of wheat falls into the earth and dies, it remains by itself alone; but if it dies, it bears much fruit" (12:23-24; italics mine).

"The hour" cannot be anything but the time of Jesus' death. It would be "the hour" He had spoken about for three years and which none of His disciples understood.

In the seventh-listed saying above, Jesus quietly lifted the edge of the shroud that hid the unimaginable results of His dying: Just as the planting of a dead grain of wheat insures a harvest of grain, so the death of the Son of God would produce a harvest of sons. *We would be born again.*

And how significant was that "hour" of which John repeatedly wrote and to which Jesus referred? Jesus continued:

"Now my soul has become troubled; and what shall I say, 'Father, save Me from this hour'? *But for this purpose I came to this hour.* Father, glorify Thy name" (Jn. 12:27-28a; italics mine).

The hour of His death was the purpose for His coming.

The synoptic gospels (Matthew, Mark, and Luke) all record one very important event that occurred just a few days before Jesus' crucifixion. We read that Peter, James, and John climbed an unnamed mountain with Jesus. There He was transfigured before them, and Matthew tells us that "His face shone like the sun, and His garments became as white as light" (Matt. 17:2).

At the same time, Moses and Elijah appeared, apparently having been taken from paradise for this special occasion. Mark tells us only that they were conversing with Jesus, but Luke tells us the subject of their conversation:

...Moses and Elijah, who, appearing in glory, *were speaking of His departure which He was about to accomplish at Jerusalem* (Lk. 9:30b-31; italics mine).

Their topic comes as no surprise, as certainly Moses and Elijah would be supremely interested in the event that would make possible the forgiveness of the sins of the world; indeed, it would be the event that made it possible for their own sins to be forgiven during their lives "on credit" of what Jesus would achieve.

It is also interesting that Luke speaks of Jesus' departure as an *accomplishment.* His death was much more than an exodus from this world.

If the reason for Jesus' conception and birth was to save people from their sins; if the purpose of His incarnation and earthly life was primarily to qualify Him to be our sinless substitute; if the Holy Spirit obviously inspired the gospel writers to spotlight the final week of Jesus' life and the events surrounding His crucifixion; and if Jesus Himself repeatedly predicted His sufferings and death, going so far as to proclaim that they were the reason He came into the world, should not we then view Christ's death as the most significant aspect of His earthly life?

FIVE

Salvation Procured

We've journeyed from before time began, when God preordained that Jesus would one day die for the sins of the world, through the centuries of preparation to the most important weekend in history. The Savior had become a man and been fully tested for thirty-three years, having lived a life of sinless perfection. Now His "hour had come." The Lamb of God was ready to be sacrificed.

On the evening before His crucifixion, Jesus gathered His disciples together to celebrate their last Passover meal together. He knew He would be dead in less than twenty-four hours, and that through His death, salvation would be procured for all who would believe. After that night, there would never again be a need for anyone to kill another Passover lamb. The Passover would be fulfilled by the sacrifice of the Lamb of God. He would be "smitten of God," and we would thus be spared the wrath we deserved. Jesus would become "Christ our Passover" (1 Cor. 5:7).

Interestingly, Jesus did not instruct His disciples to terminate their practice of the Passover. Instead, He modified the ritual to suit the revelation that His death would bring.

At His final Passover meal, He first took bread and broke it, saying it was His body that was broken for them. Next, taking a cup, He instructed them to drink from it, explaining it was His blood, the blood of the new covenant, shed for the forgiveness of sins. They were to "do this in *remembrance* of Him." The Apostle Paul later commented, "For as often as you eat this bread and drink the cup, you proclaim the Lord's death until He comes" (1 Cor. 11:23-26).

Under the old covenant, God gave numerous rites to the Israelites that He expected them to practice repeatedly. The Passover was just one example. All of these rituals served as reminders of spiritual truths and past events that God didn't want His people to forget. Their repeated practice insured that those spiritual truths and events would be consistently brought to bear on the Israelites' minds. Even if adults permitted the rituals to lapse into meaningless ceremonies, God could trust the inquisitiveness of children to evoke discussion as to the spiritual significance of what was being practiced.

For example, we read God's words in Exodus at the institution of the Passover:

> "And it will come about when your children will say to you, 'What does this rite mean to you?' that you shall say, 'It is a Passover sacrifice to the Lord who passed over the houses of the sons of Israel in Egypt when He smote the Egyptians, but spared our homes'" (Ex. 12:26-27).

A Constant Reminder

In contrast to the old covenant, under the new covenant there is only *one* ritual given that every believer should repeatedly practice throughout his Christian life—the Lord's Supper. It reveals to us the one fact, above all others, that God wants to be brought repeatedly to our minds, lest we ever let it slip away. The Lord's Supper recalls the one truth that is preeminent above all other truths. In fact, every other biblical truth is built on this truth's foundation. It is a reminder of the one event that towers over every other event in history. What is the primary significance of that singular ritual of the New Covenant?

It is a memorial to the Lord's death and a revelation of what was accomplished through His death. God wants us to remember always that Jesus died for our sins. We might neglect other important facts of the Bible, but this one fact we must never forget.

Is it any wonder that the Apostle Paul wrote, "For I delivered to you as of *first importance* what I also received, *that Christ died for our sins* according to the Scriptures..."? (1 Cor. 15:3; italics mine).

Certainly there are other wonderful truths brought to light in the Lord's Supper, but primarily it serves to remind us of Jesus' atoning sacrifice. Jesus did not institute the Lord's Supper at the beginning of His ministry—or in the middle—but at the last possible moment, just a few hours before His death. When we partake of the Lord's Supper, we should be thinking about what happened on the cross of Calvary for us.

The substitutionary aspect of Christ's death was plainly re-vealed at the last supper when Jesus gave the bread and wine to His disciples while telling them that the elements were His own body and blood. As they ate what represented the Lord's body, they were becoming one with Him. His body was thus united to their bodies, foreshadowing the blessed truth that from God's reference—when Christ died, we died with Him. We can say with Paul, "I have been crucified with Christ" (Gal. 2:20a).

Was Jesus Afraid of the Cross?

After supper, Jesus led His disciples to the Garden of Gethsemane, a place where they had frequently met. The Scripture says that "He withdrew from them about a stone's throw, and He knelt down and began to pray" (Lk. 22:41).

Next we read something that baffles those who don't under-stand what would transpire on the cross. Three times Jesus prayed a prayer that seemed so suddenly out of character:

> "Father, if Thou art willing, remove this cup from Me; yet not My will, but Thine be done" (Lk. 22:42).

This passage presents a problem. Here is the One who had never before exhibited the least bit of fear. Jesus had faced hostility, hatred, and near-death on other occasions, yet He had always remained composed. Why now was He praying, albeit predicated on God's will, that the cup He was about to drink be removed?

Even more puzzling, Luke goes on to say that,

> ...an angel from heaven appeared to Him, strengthening Him. And *being in agony* He was praying very fervently; and His sweat became like drops of blood, falling down upon the ground (Lk. 22:43-44; italics mine).

Certainly contemplating being scourged and crucified would evoke anguish in any normal human being; but was it the dreaded anticipation of those things that brought such a degree of emotional torment to Christ? Was this not why He'd been born? Was He not going to the cross because of His great love for mankind? Had He not agreed to submit to suffering and death before the world began?

Have not many Christian martyrs faced torture and death fearlessly, even with exuberance? Then why not Christ? Was He not God in the flesh? Had He become a coward?

We ask reverently: Were the two thieves who would be crucified with Jesus undergoing the same kind of agony as they considered their crucifixion? Moreover, we realize that Jesus, unlike the two thieves, knew what would happen after He died. They had to fear the unknown; Jesus didn't. He knew that on the third day He would be resurrected and ascend to His Father in glory. So why this strange episode in the garden of Gethsemane?

We must conclude there was something Jesus dreaded that was even more foreboding than the terrible agony of the cross. And there was. Something *far* more horrible.

Jesus would endure the full wrath of God Himself.

He would bear upon Himself all the guilt of the human race, accepting liability for the punishment. God's raging fury against sin would be poured out upon Him.

There is no way we could comprehend or describe the intense agony Jesus endured on the cross. If you or I could imagine all the combined torments of hell that the unsaved will suffer forever, then perhaps we could imagine what Jesus experienced during His crucifixion. The pain in His back, hands, and feet was nothing in comparison to the "anguish of His soul" of which Isaiah wrote (Is. 53:11).

What Was "the Cup"?

Jesus prayed that if God was willing, that He would "remove this cup." Of what was He speaking? What was "the cup"?

The cup to which He referred was no doubt "the cup of God's wrath," which is often mentioned in the Old Testament. For example, we read in Isaiah 51:

> Rouse yourself! Rouse yourself! Arise, O Jerusalem, you who have drunk from the Lord's hand *the cup of His anger*; the chalice of reeling you have drained to the dregs (Is. 51:17; italics mine).

God commissioned Jeremiah with a message for the nations:

> For thus the Lord, the God of Israel, says to me, "Take *this cup of the wine of wrath* from My hand, and cause all the nations, to whom I send you, to drink it. And they shall drink and stagger and go mad because of the sword that I will send among them" (Jer. 25:15-16; italics mine).

The identical expression is found in the New Testament as well. For example, we read in the book of Revelation:

> If any one worships the beast and his image, and receives a mark on his forehead or upon his hand, he also will drink of *the wine of the wrath of God, which is mixed in full strength in the cup of his anger*....And Babylon the great was remembered before God, to give her *the cup of the wine of His fierce wrath* (Rev. 14:9b-10a; 16:19b; italics mine).

The cup from which Jesus recoiled was the cup of God's terrible wrath upon sin. What you and I and every other person deserved to suffer, He suffered in our place. Jesus bore the penalty for our rebellion against God. His shed blood provided the way for God to offer us forgiveness justly.

If nothing else, Jesus' agony in the garden communicates to us that truly, just as the Bible says, "It is a terrifying thing to fall into the hands of the living God" (Heb. 10:31). Jesus was *severely* distressed at the prospect, yet He was God Himself, the "exact representation of the Father's nature" (Heb. 1:3). He was God about to suffer the wrath of God.

We might even state it this way (hopefully without raising the eyebrows of too many theologians): "What is the only thing that can frighten God?" The answer is, "Having to experience His own full wrath."

If God Himself greatly agonized over the prospect of encountering His own wrath, how much more should the person who has not yet received Christ and believed the gospel be terrified at the thought of suffering God's wrath?

Fulfilling the Father's Will

Jesus' time in the Garden of Gethsemane finally came to an end. He had resolved to fulfill His Father's will.

Then Judas the betrayer, along with a multitude of Roman soldiers and officers from the chief priests and Pharisees, arrived to arrest Him. Predictably acting on impulse, Peter drew his sword and struck the slave of the high priest, cutting off his ear in the process. Immediately Jesus commanded Peter to sheathe his sword as He amazingly healed the servant's ear.

Peter still had not grasped the fact that it was the Father's intention for Jesus to die, and, therefore, there was no point in defending Him from arrest. Jesus couldn't have made it more clear as He declared,

> "Do you think that I cannot appeal to My Father, and He will at once put at My disposal more than twelve legions of angels? How then shall the Scriptures be fulfilled, that it must happen this way?" (Matt. 26:53-54).

Jesus was not forced to go to the cross. He went by His own volition.[1] He went to fulfill the preordained, prefigured, prophesied plan of God. He went to save us from our sins. John recorded Jesus' final statement to Peter in the garden: "...the cup which the Father has given Me, shall I not drink it?" (Jn. 18:11).

Innocence on Trial

We must not consider any incident of Jesus' passion as purely incidental. Not only was His death preordained by God, but the "circumstances" that immediately preceded His execution also

---

[1] See also Jesus' statement in Jn. 10:17-18.

served a divine purpose.

We know that Jesus had numerous opportunities to be killed prior to His crucifixion, but in each case God prevented it.[2] So we ask: Was there a divine purpose for Jesus to be brought to trial before the Sanhedrin, Pontus Pilate, and Herod Antipas in the early hours of the day of His death?

As we study history in light of the Scriptures, we can certainly see the hand of God working so that His Son would have to be tried before Jewish *and* Gentile tribunals. Certainly it was not by accident that Israel was an occupied territory of the Roman Empire at the time of Christ, as those who have read Daniel's prophecies about the rise and fall of Babylon, Medo-Persia, Greece, and finally Rome have discovered. Daniel predicted that during Rome's rule the Messiah would be "cut off" (see Dan. 9:25).[3]

And was it by accident that Rome permitted the Jewish Sanhedrin to exercise its own judicial process, except in the cases of capital punishment, when Roman authorization was required? Because of this arrangement, Jesus had to be brought before Jewish *and* Gentile courts, and, for this reason, He was crucified by the Romans rather than stoned by the Jews.[4] As we will soon learn, it was imperative that Jesus die by "hanging on a tree."

And certainly it was no accident that Pontus Pilate was then governor of Judea. God had foreknown this man's cowardly character and exalted him, just as He had exalted Pharaoh of old for the fulfillment of His own divine purposes. Jesus Himself plainly spoke of God's sovereignty over Pilate's life when He said to his face, "You would have no authority over Me, unless it had been given you from above..." (Jn. 19:11a).

So what was God's purpose that His Son "be delivered up into the hands of men" as Jesus prophesied? (Mk. 9:31). Why was it necessary for Jesus to have His day in court?

Over one hundred and twenty years ago, Scottish theologian George Smeaton wrote:

> Christ was tried and sentenced at a human tribunal, which was but the visible foreground of an invisible trial in which the righteous God was judging righteously, for human guilt

[2] Lk. 4:28-30; Jn. 7:20; 8:20   [3] See also Dan. 2:1-45.   [4] See Jn. 18:31-32.

was laid upon the person of the Substitute. For wise reasons...God arranged the events of the atoning sacrifice in such a way that Christ was not to be cut off by the immediate hand of God, but by men who were His hand, and only gratifying their malice against the representative of God. The human judge [Pilate], who in the most unprecedented way absolved and yet condemned, declared Him faultless and yet passed sentence against Him, represented in the transaction the Judge of all the earth, who regarded Christ in a similar way. The human judge could only pass a sentence that would affect His body; but another sentence from a higher tribunal took effect upon His soul, and brought home the wrath of God. And under this invisible infliction the Lord experienced agony and desertion; under this He poured forth His complaint, His strong crying and tears, and endured that penal death which rescues us from the second death."[5]

Not only did Pilate and Herod find Jesus innocent,[6] but Jesus' trial before the Sanhedrin also proved His blamelessness. The record of that incident is the divine means of forever validating that Jesus was without any guilt. Why is that so important? So all who would study the story would be convinced that Jesus was crucified only for claiming to be the divine Son of God.

Cursed of God

The Apostle Paul informed us that even the mode of Jesus' execution unveiled something of its significance. In his letter to the Galatians, he quoted part of a passage from Deuteronomy 21, which says:

And if a man has committed a sin worthy of death, and he is put to death, and you hang him on a tree, his corpse shall not hang all night on the tree, but you shall surely bury him on the same day *(for he who is hanged is accursed of God)*...(Deut. 21:22-23; italics mine).

[5] George Smeaton, *The Doctrine of the Atonement According to the Apostles*, p. 182.

[6] See Lk. 23:13-15, 22; Jn. 19:4-6.

66

Paul explained that we have been redeemed from the curse—or penalty—of the law because Jesus was made a curse for us (see Gal. 3:13-14). Through the means of ordaining His Son's public hanging on a tree, God was publicly testifying to all that, according to His own Word, His innocent Son was cursed of God.

It is obvious that *if* God sent His sinless Son into the world and then permitted Him to be cruelly crucified (when God could have *easily* prevented or stopped it), then there must be a very significant reason why He did so. *Jesus was publicly exhibited as one cursed of God.*

And why would the God of perfect justice curse His sinless Son? The only possible reason, as Scripture repeatedly confirms, is because Jesus was bearing the liability for our sins.

We will bypass describing all the gory details of the act of crucifixion that Jesus endured for our sakes. However, we do take note that just before the soldiers were about to hammer the nails through Jesus' flesh, He was offered a pain-killing narcotic, wine mixed with gall, which would have considerably numbed His senses.

He innocently tasted it, but, upon realizing what it was, refused to partake. It is only natural to question why He would turn down this one act of mercy when He was, no doubt, ravaged by thirst.

We understand that Jesus came to suffer in our place, and He refused the narcotic drink because He would have nothing to do with anything that would lessen His pain or diminish His sacrifice. His faculties would not be clouded when He faced God's wrath upon sin. And so the soldiers performed their gruesome task, impaling Christ to the cross and then hoisting it up.

Through the eyes of Scripture we see Jesus hanging with a sign contemptuously posted over His head, dictated by Pilate, which read, "This is Jesus the King of the Jews" (Matt. 27:37). Just as Caiaphas, the high priest, had unwittingly prophesied before the Sanhedrin that it was expedient that one man should die on behalf of the people,[7] so Pilate had unknowingly inscribed a true title above the dying King.

That King wore a crown upon His head, not of silver or gold and

[7] Jn. 11:50; 18:14

67

precious gems, but a crown of thorns pressed into His brow. Of that hideous crown James Stalker wrote,

> Of all the features of the scene the one that has most impressed the imagination of Christendom is the crown of thorns. It was something unusual, and brought out the ingenuity and wantonness of cruelty. Besides, as the wound of a thorn has been felt by everyone, it brings the pain of our Lord nearer to us than any other incident. But it is chiefly by its symbolism that it has laid hold of the Christian mind. When Adam and Eve were driven from the garden into the bleak and toilsome world, their doom was that the ground should produce for them thorns and thistles. Thorns were the sign of the curse; that is, of their banishment from God's presence and of all the sad and painful consequences following from it....But it was the mission of Christ to bear the curse; and, as He lifted it on His own head, He took it off the world. He bore our sins and carried our sorrows.[8]

When Darkness Prevailed

Jesus was crucified at nine o'clock in the morning. Yet, after He had hung on the cross for three hours, there descended a darkness "upon all the land" (Matt. 27:45) that remained during His second three hours on the cross—from noon to three o'clock. Luke tells us the sun was obscured.

Although we are informed in the gospels of certain things that took place *before* noon—the dividing of Jesus' garments, the mocking of the bystanders, and so on—we are not told of *anything* that occurred during the three hours of darkness. What happened then is shrouded in silence as far as the four gospel writers are concerned.

From our perspective, having the revelation of the epistles, there is little doubt as to what happened. Paul wrote:

> He [God the Father] made Him [Jesus] who knew no sin to be sin on our behalf, that we might become the righteousness of God in Him (2 Cor. 5:21).

---

[8] James Stalker, *The Trial and Death of Jesus Christ*, p. 60.

Christ redeemed us from the curse of the Law, having become a curse for us—for it is written, "Cursed is every one who hangs on a tree..." (Gal. 3:13).

Obviously, these are strong metonymical expressions, as no person could literally become sin or a curse. They simply mean that Jesus bore our sin. That is, He became liable for the penalty and took the curse we deserved as sinners.

When exactly did Jesus become sin and a curse? It must have been during those three hours on the cross when darkness prevailed. At that time God poured out His judgment upon sin in the body of His Son. This mysterious period ended when Jesus' cried out, "My God, My God, why hast Thou forsaken Me?" just moments before His death (Matt. 27:46; Mk. 15:34).

Jesus' cry of dereliction only makes sense once we understand that Jesus died as our substitute. How could the One who had experienced intimate fellowship and mutual love with the Father from eternity past now cry out as one forsaken by God?

How could He, who had declared the day before, "I am not alone, because the Father is with Me" (Jn. 16:32b), now declare Himself abandoned by His Father?

The answer lies in the fact that He "bore our sins in His body on the cross," (1 Pet. 2:24a) and thus God, whose "eyes are too pure to approve evil" (Hab. 1:13) turned His back upon Him. Jesus was literally God-forsaken.

Luther's commentary on Galatians 3:13 vividly explains how Christ was made a curse for us:

> When the merciful Father saw that we were being oppressed through the Law, that we were being held under a curse, and that we could not be liberated from it by anything, He sent His Son into the world, heaped all the sins of all men upon Him, and said to Him: "Be Peter the denier; Paul the persecutor, blasphemer, and assaulter; David the adulterer; the sinner who ate the apple in Paradise; the thief on the cross. In short, be the person of all men, the one who has committed the sins of all men. And see to it that You pay and make satisfaction for them." Now comes the Law and says: "I find Him a sinner, who takes upon Himself the sins of all

men. I do not see any other sins than those in Him. Therefore let Him die on the cross!" And so it attacks Him and kills Him. By this deed the whole world is purged and expiated from all sins, and thus it is set free from death and from every evil.[9]

"It Is Finished!"

After Jesus' cry of dereliction there were only three other statements He uttered from the cross before quickly expiring.

The first was, "I am thirsty" (Jn. 19:28). Jesus was then offered and accepted some sour wine in a sponge.

The final two statements were spoken just before His final breath; the first being, "It is finished!" (Jn. 19:30).

Obviously Jesus had achieved something. What was it?

Jesus had accomplished what He had come to do—to bear our sins as our substitute. God's righteousness would be completely satisfied in just a matter of seconds when Jesus would breathe His last. Jesus had borne the full penalty. Although He would still need to be resurrected and ascend to His Father, His sufferings were finished. Salvation had been procured for all who would believe.

Then Jesus spoke His final words, crying out with a loud voice: "Father, into Thy hands I commit My Spirit" (Lk. 23:46).

Jesus was not at this point a spiritual child of Satan, as has been popularized by some. He referred to *God* as His *Father* with His last breath. His body died, and His spirit descended into Hades, the abode of the righteous and unrighteous dead, where He remained until His resurrection.

He did not descend into hell to continue suffering the torments of the damned; His sufferings ended on the cross. How could He declare "It is finished!" if He anticipated further sufferings in hell?

The Bible states that Jesus has reconciled us *"in His fleshly body through death"* (Col. 1:22). After His death, no further suffering was necessary. Jesus descended to the section of Hades known as Abraham's bosom,[10] or "Paradise," just as He had promised the repentant thief who died on a cross beside Him (see Lk. 23:43).

Further proof that Jesus did not descend into hell to continue

---

[9] Martin Luther, translated by Jaroslav Pelikan in *Luther's Works*, Vol. 26, p. 280.
[10] See Lk. 16:19-31.

suffering is found in all of the synoptic gospels. They tell us that, when Jesus cried out with His final breath, the veil in the temple dividing the holy place from the holy of holies was ripped in half from top to bottom.

The symbolism is plain: *Through His death, Jesus had provided sinful humanity access to a Holy God.* If Jesus had needed to suffer further in hell for our salvation, then, quite obviously, God would not have sent an angel to tear the temple curtain at the moment of His Son's death.

Now we've just barely passed the apex of history. Many of the mysteries that shrouded the death of Jesus to those who witnessed His sufferings have been unveiled to us. The most amazing truth is that Jesus was dying on the cross as our substitute, suffering God's judgment for our sins and fulfilling a preordained plan.

Unlike those who attended His final hours, we have the privilege of understanding the central significance of the Lord's Supper, the reason for Jesus' great agony in the garden, and the answer to why He didn't request a legion of angels to prevent His arrest. We see God's invisible tribunal represented by the earthly judge who found Jesus innocent and yet condemned Him. We can understand the necessity of His death by hanging on a tree and comprehend His refusal of the narcotic drink. In addition, the meaning of the three hours of darkness, His cry of abandonment, and His declaration of accomplishment become clear. And we can see that history can best be divided into two segments: everything that led up to the cross and everything that followed it.

Next we'll look at what happened after the cross.

Part II

After
the Cross

SIX

The Preachers Prepared

As you would suspect, in this second part we will primarily be investigating the book of Acts and the epistles. It is there we discover the full revelation of all that was accomplished through Jesus' death.

One might ask why Jesus didn't reveal all that His death would accomplish *before* He died. The answer is that He did reveal, to some degree, the significance of His death, and no doubt would have liked to explain more than He did. However, His closest friends had a difficult time even accepting that He *would* die, much less accepting any facts about what His death would accomplish.

As we survey the gospels, it is clear that no one believed Jesus would rise from the dead,[1] in spite of the fact He had promised His disciples on several occasions He would be resurrected after three days.[2] Therefore, Jesus could only feed His disciples as much truth as they could digest, and was obliged to wait until after His resurrection to reveal, through His post-resurrection appearances

[1] For example, see Mk. 16:10-14; Jn. 20:9.

[2] See Matt. 16:21; 17:22-23; 20:18-19; 26:32.

75

and the teaching ministry of the Holy Spirit, everything He desired. As Jesus said to His disciples during the Last Supper

> "I have many more things to say to you, but you cannot bear them now. But when He, the Spirit of truth, comes, He will guide you into all the truth; for He will not speak on His own initiative, but whatever He hears, He will speak; and He will disclose to you what is to come" (Jn. 16:12-13).

As we survey Acts and the Apostles' letters, we will continue our quest to uncover the necessity, significance, and centrality of the cross. It is inevitable that we'll compare the modern gospel message with the original one carried by the Apostles. But first, let's consider the events of Jesus' resurrection.

Bad Friday

As Jesus' body was taken down from the cross, no one would have ever suspected that eventually that day would be commemorated by Christians worldwide as "Good Friday." There hardly seemed to be anything good in what had transpired.

The amazing miracle-working man, the One who seemed to be Israel's long-awaited Messiah, was dead and gone. Fear, despair, and perplexity filled the hearts of the disciples. Mark tells us they were "mourning and weeping" (Mk. 16:10). The man they had faithfully followed for three years had been executed as a criminal. Incredibly, He had walked right into it. Now all hopes of establishing the long-awaited kingdom of God were dashed to pieces.

Those of us who know the end of the story can hardly appreciate the drama portrayed in the gospels. When Jesus rose from the grave on Sunday morning, first appearing at His tomb to Mary and a few other women, and later that day to Peter and the disciples, the world became a different place. Sorrow turned to joy.

Jesus made some very significant statements during His post-resurrection appearances, many of which were designed to unveil the significance of His death and resurrection. Some of those to whom Jesus spoke probably didn't initially grasp the full significance of what He said—they were just glad He was alive—but eventually the pieces began to fit together.

Christ's First Appearance

The first person to whom Jesus spoke on Sunday morning was Mary Magdalene. She was the first to discover the empty tomb but assumed Jesus' body had been stolen, adding sorrow to her sorrow. But as she stood weeping at the entrance to the tomb, suddenly Jesus appeared behind her inquiring why she was weeping and for whom she was looking (as if He didn't know!).

Never dreaming it was Jesus who was speaking to her, Mary initially thought He was the gardener. But when He called her name, Mary looked again. Realizing who He was, she cried out, "Teacher!" and fell at His feet, worshiping Him, now with tears of joy.

And then Jesus spoke:

> "Stop clinging to Me; for I have not yet ascended to the Father; but go to My brethren, and say to them, 'I ascend to My Father and your Father, and My God and your God'" (Jn. 20:17).

It seems that Mary had a grip on Jesus' feet and did not intend to let go!

Notice that Jesus referred to His disciples as *His brethren* and to His Father as *their Father*. Something had taken place in the past three days that had given the disciples a new relationship with God. Unknown to them, they had been crucified with Christ, died with Christ, been buried with Christ, and now been raised from the dead with Christ. Their sins had been cancelled out on the cross; their debt had been paid in full; they had died in Christ and now been born again in Him. They had become God's very own children, members of His family. Jesus was literally their spiritual Brother, and God was actually their spiritual Father!

This is brought out fully in the epistles. Jesus identified Himself with us, and we are, thus, vitally united with Him in His death, burial, and resurrection. He took our sin that we might have imputed to us His righteousness:

> Having concluded this, that one died for all, therefore *all died*....He made Him who knew no sin to be sin on our behalf, that we might become the righteousness of God in

Him (2 Cor. 5:14, 21).

I have been crucified with Christ; it is not longer I who live, but Christ lives in me; and the life which I now live in the flesh I live by faith in the Son of God, who loved me, and delivered Himself up for me (Gal. 2:20).

But God, being rich in mercy, because of His great love with which He loved us, even when we were dead in our transgressions, *made us alive together with Christ* (by grace you have been saved), *and raised us up with Him*, and seated us with Him in the heavenly places... (Eph. 2:4-6).

And in Him you have been made complete...*having been buried with Him in baptism, in which you were also raised up with Him* through faith in the working of God, who raised Him from the dead. And when you were dead in your transgressions...He made you *alive together with Him*, having forgiven us all our transgressions, having cancelled out the certificate of debt consisting of decrees against us and which was hostile to us; and He has taken it out of the way, having nailed it to the cross (Col. 2:10a, 12-14).

Blessed be the God and Father of our Lord Jesus Christ, who according to His great mercy *has caused us to be born again to a living hope through the resurrection of Jesus Christ from the dead*, to obtain an inheritance which is imperishable and undefiled and will not fade away, reserved in heaven for you...(1 Pet. 1:3-4).

I heard a well-known radio Bible teacher relate an incident he experienced while once touring Jerusalem with a group of Christians. They were visiting the site of the garden tomb, and their guide asked if anyone had ever been there before. This Bible teacher spoke out, "I have!" The guide then proceeded to ask him when, and he replied, "About two thousand years ago!"

Now *there* was a Bible teacher who understood his Bible! You've been there, too, if you are "in Christ." It was through Christ's death that our forgiveness was made possible, and, thus, all the other blessings we've inherited. That includes our spiritual rebirth, which in God's mind was consummated at Jesus' resurrection.

The cross was the starting place for every blessing we have in Christ. That's why they call the day He died *Good Friday*.

Explaining Things Concerning Himself

When we combine the gospel accounts of the resurrection, we find that Mary (along with a few other women), upon discovering the empty tomb, ran to inform Peter and John of her discovery and angelic vision. Mary and her friends returned to the tomb once more with Peter and John, who, upon entering, saw the empty wrappings of Jesus' body. All of them departed, but Mary lingered behind. That is when Jesus made His first appearance.[3]

His second appearance seems to have been to the other women as they returned to their homes—while Mary was still at the tomb. All we know of Jesus' conversation then is that He commanded them to instruct His disciples to leave for Galilee, promising to appear to them there.[4]

Jesus' third appearance that day was to Peter, sometime after Peter had inspected the empty tomb. However, the Bible doesn't tell us anything Jesus said during that third appearance (see Lk. 24:34; 1 Cor. 15:5).

His fourth Sunday appearance was sometime in the afternoon when He joined two disciples who were walking to the nearby village of Emmaus. In a miraculous way, they were prevented from initially recognizing Him. As they conversed, Jesus pretended to be ignorant of the events of the last three days:

> And one of them, named Cleopas, answered and said to Him, "Are you the only one visiting Jerusalem and unaware of the things which have happened here in these days?" And He said to them, "What things?" And they said to Him, "The things about Jesus the Nazarene, who was a prophet mighty in deed and word in the sight of God and all the people, and how the chief priests and our rulers delivered Him up to the sentence of death, and crucified Him. But we were hoping that it was He who was going to redeem Israel. Indeed, besides all this, it is the third day since these things hap-

[3] See Jn. 20:1-18.   [4] See Matt. 28:9-10.

pened. But also some women among us amazed us. When they were at the tomb early in the morning, and did not find His body, they came, saying that they had also seen a vision of angels, who said that He was alive. And some of those who were with us went to the tomb and found it just exactly as the women also had said; but Him they did not see" (Lk. 24:18-24).

These men should have been rejoicing that the Old Testament predictions of the Messiah's sufferings and resurrection had been fulfilled, but unfortunately their knowledge of those predictions was sorely deficient. Jesus then responded to their perplexity:

"O foolish men and slow of heart to believe in all that the prophets have spoken! Was it not necessary for the Christ to suffer these things and to enter into His glory?" And beginning with Moses and with all the prophets, He explained to them the things concerning Himself in all the Scriptures (Lk. 24:25-27).

What a sensational Bible study that must have been! The two disciples later reminisced, "Were not our hearts burning within us while He was speaking to us on the road, while He was explaining the Scriptures to us?" (Lk. 24:32).

How their faces must have lit up as it gradually dawned on them that Jesus' death and resurrection was God's predetermined plan! And when their "eyes were opened" to recognize that it was Jesus who was speaking to them, He suddenly vanished. They immediately hurried back to Jerusalem to tell the other disciples.

This fourth appearance is very significant because it was then that Jesus began His post-resurrection teaching ministry. These two disciples were privileged to learn of numerous messianic references in the Old Testament. In fact, Jesus was particularly interested in enlightening them to scriptures that predicted His sufferings and resurrection. Jesus was preparing His disciples to preach the gospel, and those scriptures would be the basis of their preaching.

According to the Scriptures

Jesus' final Sunday appearance was that evening when He

suddenly stood in the midst of the disciples who were hiding "for fear of the Jews" (Jn. 20:19).

He greeted their surprise by saying, "Peace to you", and then "reproached them for their hardness of heart, because they had not believed those who had seen Him after He had risen " (Mk. 16:14).

Again we find Jesus making reference to the prophecies He fulfilled in His death and resurrection:

> Now He said to them, "These are My words which I spoke to you while I was still with you, that all things which are written about Me in the Law of Moses and the Prophets and the Psalms must be fulfilled." Then He opened their minds to understand the Scriptures, and He said to them, "Thus it is written, that the Christ should suffer and rise again from the dead the third day; and that repentance for forgiveness of sins should be proclaimed in His name to all nations, beginning in Jerusalem" (Lk. 24:44-47).

The phrase, "Then He opened their minds to understand the Scriptures," is certainly intriguing. Either Jesus supernaturally gave them instant understanding of the Old Testament messianic types and prophecies, or, more likely, He went through all the Scriptures, explaining them, just as He had done with the two disciples on the road to Emmaus.

Regardless, more than anything else, Jesus wanted His disciples to understand that His death and resurrection were foreordained by God and that now repentance for forgiveness of sins could be proclaimed in His name. Within a few weeks, Jesus would commission His disciples to take the gospel to the entire world, and, of necessity, they must have a clear understanding of what that gospel is.

It is of equal importance that we understand these fundamental truths as well. Yet I'm concerned that many people, and even some pastors, have forgotten or neglected these foundational truths. When a preacher invites people to accept Jesus with the enticement of a better life and some peace of mind but never mentions Christ's death, resurrection, or the forgiveness of sins, then he has not, according to biblical standards, preached the gospel. And unless he preaches the authentic gospel, how can people be authentically saved?

As we survey the book of Acts, we will notice again and again that the core of the apostles' message was Christ's death and resurrection. And we will see how they repeatedly appealed to the Old Testament scriptures that predicted Jesus' death and resurrection as proof that Jesus was indeed the Savior. This is the foundation of our faith, just as the Apostle Paul wrote:

> For I delivered to you as of *first importance* what I also received, that Christ died for our sins *according to the Scriptures,* and that He was buried, and that He was raised on the third day *according to the Scriptures*...(1 Cor. 15:3-4).

Notice Paul appealed to the Scriptures twice: once for the death and once for the resurrection of Christ.

The Great Commission

Jesus made a number of other appearances after the initial five on the day of His resurrection. We are told by Luke (in the book of Acts) that Jesus appeared to the apostles "over a period of forty days," "speaking of the things concerning the kingdom of God" (Acts 1:3).

It was sometime during those appearances that Jesus commissioned His disciples to take the gospel to every nation. Significantly, on at least two occasions, Jesus commanded the apostles to baptize their converts (see Matt. 28:19; Mk. 16:16).

When we read through the book of Acts, we find that the apostles consistently obeyed Jesus' instruction, immediately baptizing anyone who professed Christ. This is much more important than many today realize, which is why so many who are ministers don't *quickly* baptize new believers, and why some *never* do.

Why did Jesus command the baptism of new believers? There are several reasons, but one often overlooked is that baptism *should* insure that preachers *will* preach the true gospel, and that converts *will understand* the true message of the gospel.

Baptism is representative of the believer's identification with Jesus' death, burial, and resurrection (see Col. 2:10-14; Rom. 6:3-

11). In hearing the gospel, a person *should* hear about Christ's death and resurrection and that Jesus was his substitute, identifying Himself with sinners so they might be justly forgiven. Baptism then provides the new believer a "corresponding action" to express his faith in the message he has heard. Through baptism, he is saying, "I believe that Jesus identified with me, and from now on I identify myself with Him."

Why is it that so many of us who preach "the gospel" don't invite those who say they believe in Christ to be baptized immediately? Simply because baptism isn't a logical end to our message. It would make no sense to the new "convert" because he hasn't heard the true gospel of Jesus' substitutionary death and His resurrection.

When we proclaim the true gospel, it should come as no surprise if those who want to be saved respond with the words (as did the Ethiopian eunuch of Acts 8 who heard the gospel from Philip's lips): "Look! Water! What prevents me from being baptized?" (Acts 8:36). But how many of our new converts, if we instructed them to be baptized, would respond, "Whatever for?"

Only when the authentic gospel is proclaimed will they understand why they should be baptized, because only then will they understand the significance of Jesus' death and resurrection.

In the next chapter, we'll further compare our modern methods with those of the apostles whom Christ commissioned.

SEVEN

The Cross Proclaimed

The apostles proclaimed a message radically different from the so-called gospel message prevalent in many "evangelical"[1] churches today. Too often, the *biblical* gospel has been replaced by a modern gospel that is void of practically every essential biblical element.

This modern gospel proclaims, "Accept Jesus and get a better life." The listeners are reminded of their temporal problems and then offered peace of mind and a relationship with God. They are promised that God will begin to do things for them if they will only "invite Jesus into their hearts."

No mention is made of sin or of the necessity and accomplishment of the cross; whereas the authentic gospel is, as Paul stated, "*the word of the cross*" (1 Cor. 1:18; italics mine).

No invitation to be baptized is made because it would make no sense. Baptism is something for Christians to consider only when the annual baptismal service takes place.

[1] By "evangelical" I'm referring to any church where people claim to be "born again."

85

No one is told to repent of sin simply because it doesn't fit into the message. "God is love—invite Him into your life and things will start getting better."

Whatever Happened to Repentance?

I well remember the first time I did a word study, using a concordance, of *repentance* in the New Testament. How surprised I was to discover that repentance is essential for salvation and part of the gospel message! It was then that I began to realize how defective my own gospel really was.

When the true gospel is proclaimed, repentance naturally makes sense to the hearers. If Jesus suffered incomprehensible agony on the cross, being punished in my place for my sins, then it stands to reason that if I'm going to begin a relationship with God, I cannot continue sinning as I always have.

But repentance is foreign to the "accept Jesus and get a better life" gospel. The listener is told that God wants to bless him and fulfill his every desire. God will make him rich and give him joy and peace in the midst of a troubled world. He doesn't need to repent of greed, which the Bible says is idolatry,[2] because God wants to give him more success and bigger cars and homes. God will make him happy and give him greater self-esteem.

But this is not the gospel of the New Testament. Although God certainly does want to bless and prosper *His children,* a person can only become one of God's children if he repents and believes in the Jesus who died for his sins. That is what the Bible teaches.

Did the apostles preach the gospel by telling the unsaved that God wanted to bless them? Peter *once* did, at the end of his second sermon recorded in the third chapter of Acts. But listen to how he said it:

> "For you, first, God raised up His servant, and *sent Him to bless you by turning every one of you from your wicked ways*." (Acts 3:26; italics mine).

God wants to bless everyone, but His blessings begin with each individual's repentance. God wants people to "turn from their wicked ways."

[2] Col. 3:5

I remember an evangelist who once visited our city and brought with him the vice-president of a major mid-western beer brewery. He introduced his guest as a "Spirit-filled Christian who was a missionary to his beer company"!

How absurd! Here was a man who made his living producing a product responsible for thousands of broken marriages and homes, thousands of innocent deaths and permanent disabilities, untold suffering and disease, and higher insurance rates for everyone, yet he claims to be a believer in Jesus Christ! And all under the guise of being a missionary to the other hell-bound people who worked for the same company!

Should a man who runs a house of prostitution keep his place open for business-as-usual once he believes in Jesus so he can be a missionary to prostitutes and those who pay for their services?

Should a drug lord, once he believes in Jesus, continue to smuggle drugs, extort politicians, and "rub-off" his competitors in order to be a missionary to the drug pushers?

If the vice-president of that brewery was truly saved and wanted to reach his employees for Christ, he should have sent them all a memo saying, "I've decided to follow Jesus who died for me, a wicked sinner. My job at this brewery is not compatible with what is right, as we all know, and so I resign, effective immediately."

The Churches' First Sermon

The book of Acts contains material crucial to our study of the cross. By examining the content of the gospel messages proclaimed by the early church, we can compare the gospel we read with the gospel we have heard (or preached). For the most part, we will only study incidents where actual portions of gospel sermons are recorded for us. There are other cases in the book of Acts where we are simply told that so-and-so "preached the gospel," but the actual content of the message is not recorded.

The Apostle Peter preached the first gospel sermon of the church on the day of Pentecost. Did he tell his listeners that God would begin to solve their temporal problems if they would only invite Jesus into their hearts? No, Peter had listened well to Jesus' post-resurrection instructions because he preached that all people are sinners (2:38,40), that Jesus died on the cross (2:23, 36), that

87

Jesus' death was predetermined by God (2:23), and that Jesus had been resurrected according to the Scripture (2:24-32). Also included in his message was the necessity of repentance (2:38), the need to be baptized (2:38), and that the primary benefit of salvation was the forgiveness of sins (2:38).

Peter quoted from Psalm 16:8-11 to prove that the resurrection of the Messiah had been prophetically predicted. Undoubtedly, this was one of the scriptures Jesus had identified to the Emmaus road disciples (and probably to the other disciples as well).

Peter argued that David (the author of Psalm 16) could not be referring to himself as the "holy one" whom God did not allow to "undergo decay," because David had died and was buried, and his tomb was with them "until this day" (Acts 2:27-29). David must have been prophesying concerning the resurrection of Christ.

Peter also quoted a portion of Psalm 110 (also authored by David) as referring to Jesus' ascension to the right hand of God the Father.

It is notable that Peter's listeners were "pierced to the heart" when they heard his sermon. This should be normal when the gospel is preached. The Holy Spirit, Jesus promised, would "convict the world concerning sin" (Jn. 16:8). If our gospel has no convicting power, then it isn't the authentic gospel.

The Essential Elements

We must question whether or not Luke recorded every word of the sermons he reported in the book of Acts. More than likely, he did not and instead only recorded the main points. If, then, we find an essential element of the gospel missing in one of the sermons, there's no need to conclude it was not part of the original message.

Peter's second sermon, after the healing of the cripple at the Beautiful Gate, included the elements of humanity's guilt (3:13-15, 19, 26), God's wrath (3:23), the death of Christ (3:15), the prediction of His sufferings by the prophets (3:18, 24), His resurrection (3:15, 26), the necessity of repentance for salvation (3:19), and the fact that the forgiveness of sins was now being offered through Christ (3:19). Of the seven essential elements contained in Peter's first sermon, only baptism is not included in his second sermon (or more likely, not recorded by Luke).

Peter also quoted two Old Testament passages as being fulfilled by Jesus: Moses' prediction that God would raise up a prophet like himself (Deut. 18:15), and God's promise to Abraham that all the families of the earth would be blessed through his seed (Gen. 22:18).

Jesus must have mentioned these two scriptures during His discourse with the Emmaus road disciples and probably with the others later. Naturally, the Old Testament scripture quotations were the most effective when the gospel was being proclaimed to Jews rather than Gentiles.

Peter's sermon *obviously* had an impact on his listeners because "many of those who had heard the message believed; and the number of the men came to be about five thousand" (Acts 4:4). Imagine that!

How to Preach the Gospel

Unlike Peter, some preachers today consider it inappropriate to mention humanity's sinfulness, God's wrath, or the necessity of repentance when they proclaim the gospel. I remember once speaking to a group of pastors in a foreign country who had swallowed this kind of unbiblical thinking. They had been told by their "apostle" never to mention sin or God's wrath when preaching the gospel because it would "turn people off" to Christianity. (These were full-gospel, charismatic, evangelical pastors!) And they believed it!

But if humanity is not sinful, then Christ's death is meaningless, seeing that He died for our sins. *The true gospel cannot be preached without mention of humanity's guilt.*

If you will take the time to study great revivals of the past, you will soon see that the preachers of the gospel during those awakenings expounded a message that *first* convicted people of their sins.

The successful Methodist evangelist and circuit rider of the "Second Great Awakening," Francis Asbury, along with Bishop Coke, in the 1798 *Methodist Discipline*, encouraged their fellow-preachers to

> Convince the sinner of his dangerous condition....He must set forth the depth of original sin, and shew the sinner how

far he is gone from original righteousness; he must describe the vices of the world in their just and most striking colors, and enter into all the sinner's pleas and excuses for sin, and drive him from all his subterfuges and strongholds.[3]

In his landmark book, *Revivals of Religion,* in a chapter entitled "How to Preach the Gospel," anointed revivalist Charles Finney wrote,

> It is of great importance that the sinner should be made to *feel his guilt*....Sinners ought to be made to feel that they have *something* to do, and that is, *to repent*....Sinners should be made to feel that if they *now* grieve away the Spirit of God, it is very probable that they will be *lost forever*."[4]

Legendary Baptist preacher, C. H. Spurgeon, told those preparing for ministry:

> The preaching of the cross is to them that are saved the wisdom of God and the power of God. The Christian minister should preach all the truths which cluster around the person and work of the Lord Jesus, and hence he must declare very earnestly and pointedly *the evil of sin,* which created the need of a Savior. Let him show that sin is a breach of the law, that it necessitates punishment, and that the wrath of God is revealed against it....Open up the spirituality of the law as our Lord did, and show how it is broken by evil thoughts, intents, and imaginations. By this means sinners will be pricked in their hearts.

> Old Robbie Flockhart used to say, "It is of no use trying to sew with the silken thread of the gospel unless we pierce a way for it with the sharp needle of the law." The law goes first, like the needle, and draws the gospel thread after it; therefore preach concerning sin, righteousness, and the judgment to come....Aim at the heart. Probe the wound and touch the very quick of the soul. Spare not the sterner themes, for men must be wounded before they can be healed,

[3] Francis Asbury, as quoted by L.C. Rudolph in *Francis Asbury,* p. 154.

[4] Charles G. Finney, *Revivals of Religion,* pp. 205-7.

and slain before they can be made alive. No man will ever put on the robe of Christ's righteousness till he is stripped of his fig leaves, nor will he wash in the fount of mercy till he perceives his filthiness....We must also set before our hearers the justice of God and *the certainty that every transgression will be punished.*"[5]

As Spurgeon declared, not only must we preach humanity's guilt, but also God's wrath against sin. If God is not wrathful, then, again, Christ's death is meaningless on two counts.

First, if God is not wrathful, then there was no reason for Jesus to die because there is no hell, there is nothing for people to be saved from, and no one need be concerned about future punishment.

As R.W. Dale succinctly wrote, "One of the chief reasons why men do not trust in Christ to save them, is that they do not believe that there is anything from which they need to be saved."[6]

And second, if God is not wrathful, then Jesus *did not* suffer God's wrath on the cross. He was not humanity's substitute, and no atonement took place for our sins. If God is not a God of wrath, then the gospel of the New Testament is simply not true.

Proclaiming Christ

As we continue to survey Acts, let us look not only for the preaching of the death and resurrection of Christ but also for the proclamation of humanity's guilt and God's holiness and wrath. The very fact that forgiveness of sins is offered through the gospel makes it obvious to any intelligent listener that humanity is guilty and God is wrathful, otherwise forgiveness of sins is irrelevant. When we say we have been "saved" or have experienced "salvation," we are affirming both our guilt and God's wrath, as it is God's just wrath from which we have been saved (see Rom. 5:9).

In Peter and John's short defense before the Sanhedrin (Acts 4:1-22), Peter, speaking by the Holy Spirit, proclaimed Christ's death, His resurrection, and that salvation could come only through Him (Acts 4:10-12).

[5] C.H. Spurgeon, *Lectures to My Students*, p. 181.
[6] R.W. Dale, *The Atonement*, p. 348.

Peter again appealed to Scripture, quoting Psalm 118:22, saying that Jesus was the stone whom the builders rejected, but which became the very corner stone. Again, this probably was an Old Testament reference he learned from Jesus.

In Peter and the apostles' four-sentence defense before the Sanhedrin in Acts 5, they were able to include Christ's death on the cross, His resurrection, the need for repentance, and the benefit of forgiveness of sins (Acts 5:29-32).

After the persecution of the church following the martyrdom of Stephen, Philip journeyed thirty-five miles north of Jerusalem to preach the gospel to the people of Samaria. Luke didn't record any of his actual sermons but simply wrote that Philip was "proclaiming Christ to them" (Acts 8:5)

I don't think that Philip stood and just repeated, "Christ! Christ! Christ! Christ!" over and over again! No, he proclaimed that Jesus had died on the cross, was resurrected, and that, through Him, forgiveness of sins was available to all who repented and believed. This must have been the case because Philip immediately baptized all his converts (Acts 8:12-13). The believers wanted to identify with the One who had identified Himself with them.

After the "Samaria crusade," Philip was instructed by an angel to journey to the road that descends from Jerusalem to Gaza, where he crossed paths with an Ethiopian eunuch traveling in his chariot. Providentially, the eunuch was reading from the fifty-third chapter of Isaiah when he met Philip, and he asked him to explain what he had been reading.

There could have been no better scripture in the Old Testament from which to preach the gospel! Isaiah 53 includes the truths of humanity's guilt (53:5-6, 11-12), God's wrath (53:4-6, 10), Christ's atoning death (53:4-12), (obviously) the preordination of Christ's death, and His resurrection (53:10, 12).

Luke recorded Philip's response to the eunuch's question: "And Philip opened his mouth, and beginning from this Scripture he preached Jesus to him" (Acts 8:35).

Philip evidently presented the message of the cross so effectively that the eunuch himself asked to be baptized when he spotted water along the road. He had heard the good news that Jesus had died for his sins on the cross and wanted to identify with the One who had identified with him. The eunuch confessed he believed that Jesus Christ is the Son of God, and then Philip immediately baptized him (see Acts 8:36-38).

Why Mention Judgment?

In the tenth chapter of Acts we find the narrative of the first preaching of the gospel to the Gentiles. Having been supernaturally directed to journey to Caesarea to the home of Cornelius, Peter found this Roman centurion "who feared God with all his household" (Acts 10:2).

Speaking to Cornelius and his family and servants, Peter proclaimed that Jesus had performed miracles by the power of God (10:38), that He had died on a cross (10:39), that He had risen on the third day and had been seen by many people (10:40-41), that He had been appointed by God "as Judge of the living and the dead" (10:42), that the prophets had spoken of Him (10:43), and that everyone who believes in Him receives forgiveness of sins (10:43).

Obviously the truths of humanity's guilt and God's wrath were implied in Peter's sermon as he mentioned that Jesus had been appointed by God as Judge of the living and the dead and that He was now offering forgiveness of sins.

Interestingly, we learn in this passage of Scripture something that Jesus *commanded* His apostles to proclaim, which heretofore had not been revealed. Peter stated that Jesus "ordered us to preach to the people, and solemnly to testify that this is the One who has been appointed by God as Judge of the living and the dead" (Acts 10:42).

Thus we can confidently say that the proclamation that "Jesus is God's appointed Judge" is a part of the gospel. The clear implication is that there is a future judgment coming when all people will be judged. If people are going to be judged, then obviously there are rewards and punishments, otherwise judgment is meaningless.

Can you see that if there is no future judgment, then Christ's death, again, is meaningless? If there is no future judgment, then there was no reason for Jesus to die because there is no hell to escape or heaven to gain. Proclaiming the future judgment is a part of proclaiming the gospel. The Apostle Paul affirmed this in his letter to the Romans:

> ...on the day when, *according to my gospel*, God will judge the secrets of men through Christ Jesus (Rom. 2:16; italics mine).

The future judgment is something we can and should mention when we proclaim the gospel.

Can you see how this gospel differs dramatically from the "accept Jesus and get a better life" gospel? *The primary reason that people should come to Jesus is because they understand that they desperately need their sins forgiven and that forgiveness is only possible through Jesus and His atoning sacrifice.* Thus, people need to be aware of their need before they will respond to the gospel. Our preaching should help people see their need for a Savior.

The only thing people believe when they hear the "accept Jesus and get a better life gospel" is that if they invite Jesus into their heart, they will get a better life. This is why many of those "converts" stop attending church and fall away from God once their life improves (or doesn't improve).

For years I wondered why some of my converts were so unfaithful and seemed uninterested in growing in God. The reason was because they initially came to God to improve their situation in life—to make more money, to repair their marriage, to develop good friendships, and so on. Certainly God will provide those things for His children, but people should come to God to have their sins forgiven and to escape the wrath they deserve, which Jesus endured in their place on the cross. That is the starting place.

Preaching Christ Crucified

In addition to Peter's sermons, Luke recorded several of the Apostle Paul's gospel messages. In Acts 13, we read about Paul's preaching to the Jews in a synagogue in Pisidian Antioch. His sermon (as I'm sure you expected by now) included the mention of Jesus' death on the cross (13:27-30), His resurrection and appearance to many witnesses (13:30-37), His fulfillment of the predictions of the prophets (particularly in His resurrection) (13:23, 27, 33-37), and that through Him forgiveness of sins is offered (13:38). Paul concluded his sermon by quoting from the prophet Habakkuk a warning of God's judgment that is directed at those who will not believe in God's amazing work (13:41).

In his sermon, Paul quoted portions of Psalms 2 and 16, and Isaiah 55, to prove that the Messiah's resurrection had been predicted by the prophets.

In Acts 17 we read of Paul's preaching to Jews in Thessalonica, and although Luke did not record Paul's sermons there, he does mention their general content:

> And according to Paul's custom, he went to them, and for three Sabbaths reasoned with them from the Scriptures, explaining and giving evidence that *the Christ had to suffer and rise again from the dead*, and saying, "This Jesus whom I am proclaiming to you is the Christ" (Acts 17:2-3; italics mine).

Paul concentrated on proving from the Old Testament (as we call it) that the Messiah had to suffer, die, and rise from the dead.

In Athens we find Paul speaking to *Gentiles*, "preaching Jesus and the resurrection" (Acts 17:18). Paul did alter his message somewhat. He first laid a basic foundation about God that would be unnecessary for a Jewish audience. Then he noticeably excluded any reference to Old Testament messianic predictions that would have been all but meaningless to his Gentile hearers. Still, Paul included the essential elements of the gospel:

> "Therefore having overlooked the times of ignorance, God is now declaring to men that all everywhere should *repent*, because He has fixed a day in which *He will judge the world in righteousness through a Man* whom He has appointed, having furnished proof to all men by *raising Him from the dead*." (Acts 17:30-31; italics mine).

I wonder, if he were alive today, if Paul would be criticized by some modern ministers for preaching such a negative message. They might tell him not to mention God's future judgment and that repentance is not a requirement to be saved—it is only a doctrine preached by legalists!

Paul, on many occasions, did face opposition to his "narrow-minded" message, but that never deterred him from preaching the truth. In the next chapter of Acts (chapter 18) we read of Paul journeying to Corinth, where he remained for eighteen months. Again, we have no record of Paul's actual sermons, but we do know what he preached there from reading his later letter to the Christians in Corinth:

> For I determined to know nothing among you except *Jesus Christ, and Him crucified* (1 Cor. 2:2; italics mine).

He also testified in the same letter,

> For indeed Jews ask for signs, and Greeks search for wisdom; but *we preach Christ crucified,* to Jews a stumbling block, and to Gentiles foolishness, but to those who are the called, both Jews and Greeks, Christ the power of God and the Wisdom of God (1 Cor. 1:22-24; italics mine).

And reminding them of his initial message, Paul said,

> Now I make known to you, brethren, the gospel which I preached to you....For I delivered to you as of first importance what I also received, that *Christ died for our sins* according to the Scriptures, and that He was buried, and that He was raised on the third day according to the Scriptures (1 Cor. 15:1, 3-4; italics mine).

The content of Paul's messages in Corinth underscores his conviction to proclaim the true gospel without wavering.

A Convicting Message

Paul's imprisonment in Caesarea provided opportunities for him to personally share the gospel. His meetings with Felix, governor of Judea, and King Herod Agrippa II are recorded by Luke in the final chapters of Acts.

Paul discussed four subjects with Felix, a man whom history records as "indulging in every kind of barbarity and lust, [who] exercised the power of a king in the spirit of a slave."[7]

---

[7] As so said the Roman historian Tacitus in his *Histories* V, 9.

The four topics Paul discussed with him were (1) faith in Jesus Christ, (2) righteousness, (3) self-control, and (4) the judgment to come (see Acts 24:24-25). Even before this, the Bible tells us that Felix had a knowledge of "the Way" and, therefore, had already been exposed to the gospel (see Acts 24:22).

Paul discussed "faith in Jesus Christ" because that is how a person is saved.

He discussed "righteousness" because the gospel reveals God's righteousness (see Rom. 1:17). God righteously punished the sins of the world in Christ. And as a result of believing the gospel, we are said to be made "the righteousness of God in Christ" (2 Cor. 5:21).

Third, Paul discussed "self-control." Was Paul advising Felix how to lose weight if he'd only exercise self-control? No, he was discussing the fact that all people are out-of-control sinners who need a Savior.

And fourth, Paul discussed "the judgment to come." That is, all people will have to stand before God's judgment seat one day, and if they have not received on earth the pardon God offered them through Christ, then they will be eternally confined to hell. All these things Paul shared with an unsaved person.

The result was that Felix "became frightened" (Acts 24:25) and dismissed Paul from his presence.

Why was Felix so frightened? I think it is safe to say that He was convicted by the Holy Spirit. Of what does the Holy Spirit convict people? Listen to what Jesus said:

> "And He [the Holy Spirit], when He comes, will convict the world concerning *sin*, and *righteousness*, and *judgment*; concerning sin, because they do not believe in Me..." (Jn. 16:8-9; italics mine).

Is it any wonder that Paul spoke to Felix about the very things Jesus had promised the Holy Spirit would convict people?

If the Holy Spirit will convict people of sin, righteousness, and judgment, then we ought to be speaking of those things to unbelievers. It is obvious that the Holy Spirit does not do our work for us—He *helps* us do our work. He'll only convict people of those things when we speak of them.

I've seen unsaved people come under so much conviction when they heard the authentic gospel preached that they literally shook. And they should have! But I can guarantee that you won't find anyone shaking in his seat when he hears the "accept Jesus and get a better life" gospel!

Again, I can't help but wonder how Paul might have been criticized if he were alive today and shared the gospel in the same manner as he did with Felix. How many would call him too negative or a "hell-fire and brimstone" or "gloom and doom" preacher?

Lastly, Paul was given opportunity to defend himself before King Agrippa, the grandson of the man who ordered the slaughter of Bethlehem's babies, and the son of the man who had martyred the Apostle James.

In Paul's defense before this ungodly king, he mentions humanity's guilt (26:18), Christ's sufferings and death (26:23), His resurrection (26:8, 15-16, 23), the prediction by the prophets of Christ's sufferings (26:22, 27), the forgiveness of sins made possible through Christ (26:18), and the necessity of repentance and faith for salvation (26:18, 20). Did you expect anything less?

The Importance of the Resurrection

It has been observed by many that the apostles seemed to emphasize Christ's resurrection above all else in their proclamation of the gospel. Certainly the resurrection is emphasized as much as Christ's death on the cross. (And of course, if Jesus hadn't died, He could not have been raised.) Why is the resurrection so important?

The resurrection is vital for several reasons. Most importantly, Jesus' resurrection proved that the penalty for our sin had been paid in full because Jesus was no longer under the wrath of God. God's justice had been satisfied; thus death could no longer hold Him. As Paul also wrote in his letter to the Romans:

> He [Jesus] who was delivered up because of our transgressions, and was raised because of our justification (Rom. 4:25).

Thomas J. Crawford (quoting a Mr. Horsley), wrote concerning this passage:

> We had sinned—*therefore* the Savior died; our justification was secured by His obedience unto death—*therefore* He was raised again from the dead. I may add, that this interpretation of the latter clause throws light on an otherwise obscure statement of the same apostle, 1 Cor. 15:17, "If Christ be not raised, your faith is vain, ye are yet in your sins;" that is to say, "If Christ be not raised, you have no ground for trusting that His death has been accepted as an effectual atonement for you."[8]

Second, the doctrine of the resurrection is important simply because the message of Jesus' substitutionary death on the cross is not very convincing if Jesus remained dead. When we hear of criminals who are executed in the electric chair or gas chamber, we don't normally think of them as dying for our sins but for their own!

Can you imagine the reaction of people in that day if they heard someone saying that Jesus had been executed by the Roman authorities, and now He, though dead, was offering them forgiveness for their sins? How can a dead criminal save anyone?

But if we proclaim that Jesus was raised from the dead on the third day and was seen by many witnesses, then *obviously* His death on the cross had some significance. This person who died on the cross must be somebody special.

Unfortunately, our culture has become numb to the message of Christ's resurrection, due partly to the fact that practically everyone has heard the Easter story over and over again or been exposed in some way to what is commemorated on Easter Sunday. People never stop to think about how incredible it was that Jesus repeatedly predicted His death by crucifixion and His resurrection after three days, and then actually pulled it off!

If Jesus really did rise from the dead, then we ought to listen to everything He had to say, before and after His resurrection. The resurrection was in a class by itself compared to other miracles— it authenticated Christ's deity like nothing else. Just as the Apostle Paul wrote in the introduction to his letter to the Romans:

[8] Thomas J. Crawford, *The Doctrine of the Holy Scripture Respecting the Atonement*, pp. 27-28.

Christ Jesus...who was declared the Son of God with power by the resurrection from the dead... (Rom. 1:1a, 4a).

And third, the fact of the resurrection was also essential to validate the apostles' claim that God had appointed Jesus as Judge of the living and the dead (which is something Jesus ordered the apostles to preach—see Acts 10:42). How could a dead man judge anyone?

How's Your Gospel?

When we began our survey of Acts, I realized it might become a bit tedious to repeatedly read that the same consistent message was proclaimed by the early apostles. But I wanted you to see that the true gospel message contains several essential elements—some of which have been edited from the gospel we so often hear today.

We must never forget, as Jesus Himself said, that His blood was shed for the forgiveness of sins (Matt. 26:28). Our gospel, above all else, offers people *forgiveness for their sins.* Therefore, we should not think that mentioning humanity's sinfulness, God's wrath, or the future judgment is incompatible with preaching the gospel. Yes, God has an inheritance for those who are saved, and we can receive more from God than forgiveness. But forgiveness is the starting place. Only one who is forgiven can receive God's other blessings.

Of course, there are those who only preach about humanity's sins and God's judgment, never offering anyone the solution, which is the message of Jesus' death on the cross. That, too, is a terrible extreme. We should preach a balanced gospel, emphasizing certain aspects as the Holy Spirit directs us to tailor our message to certain audiences but never completely excluding any essential element.

So here is a summary of the gospel presented in Acts:

"Jesus was a man sent by God, attested by the many miracles He performed. Yet He was condemned and crucified by evil men, but in so doing, He fulfilled the preordained plan of God, because the ancient prophets predicted His sufferings and death. After three days, He rose from the dead and was seen by many witnesses; this, too, was predicted by the prophets. Now He has commanded us to preach that men everywhere should repent, because He will one day judge every person. He is offering to all the forgiveness of their sins. So repent, believe in Him, and be baptized in His name."

How does your gospel square up with that?

EIGHT

The Cross Preeminent

It's a fact: The cross of Jesus Christ and the topics directly related to it dominate the epistles of the New Testament. George Smeaton, observing this fact in the writings of the apostles to the early Christians, notes how often they refer to Christ's atoning death:

> The numerous explanations they [the epistles] contain as to the Lord's atoning death, suffice to prove that there is not a spiritual blessing which does not stand in immediate or mediate connection with it, not a duty which is not enforced by it as a motive. How wide the influence of this great article is on doctrine and practice, at once appears from the place which it occupies in the epistles. The entire range of Scripture truth takes a tincture from it, and its influence is felt even where it may not be expressly named.[1]

Of the approximate 2,759 sentences in the epistles,[2] we find that

[1] George Smeaton, *The Doctrine of the Atonement*, p. 100.

[2] This is based upon the *New American Standard* version.

ninety contain a direct reference to Christ's death, crucifixion, blood, or cross. That amounts to one out of every thirty-one sentences.[3]

If we then add to our list other uncounted sentences that speak of "the gospel" (which is "the word of the cross"[4]) and those mentioning Jesus as "the Lamb" (an obvious reference to His sacrificial death on the cross), then *one out of every sixteen sentences* makes reference to Christ's death on the cross.[5]

Finally, if we add further uncounted sentences that make some direct reference to Jesus' death in words other than those mentioned above—in such phrases as "He offered Himself," "laid down His life," "gave Himself," or "sacrifice of Himself," and so on—then *one out of every thirteen sentences in the epistles makes some reference to Jesus' death on the cross.*[6]

It would be well for those of us who preach God's Word to

[3] See Rom. 1:4; 3:25; 4:24; 5:6, 8, 9, 10; 6:3, 4, 5-6, 8-9, 10; 7:4; 8:11, 34; 10:7, 9; 14:9, 15; 1 Cor. 1:17, 18, 23; 2:2, 8; 8:11; 10:16; 11:25, 26, 27; 15:3, 20; 2 Cor. 4:10; 5:14-15; 13:4; Gal. 1:1; 2:20, 21; 3:1; 5:11; 6:12, 14; Eph. 1:7, 20; 2:13, 16; Phil. 2:8; 3:10; Col. 1:18, 20, 22; 2:12, 14, 20; 1 Thes. 1:10; 2:15; 4:14; 5:10; 2 Tim. 2:8, 11, Heb. 2:9, 14; 5:7; 6:6; 9:12, 14, 15; 10:19, 29; 12:2, 24; 13:12, 20; 1 Pet. 1:2, 3, 19, 21; 2:24; 3:18; 1 Jn. 1:7; 5:6, 8; Rev. 1:5, 5, 18; 2:8; 5:9; 7:14; 11:8; 12:11; 19:13.

[4] Today, "the gospel" is a loosely-used term in many circles, unfortunately used to label any kind of positive preaching. But the phrase "the gospel" in the New Testament refers strictly to the message of Christ's atoning death on the cross, His burial, and His resurrection; see 1 Cor. 15:1-5.

[5] See Rom. 1:4, 9, 15, 16; 2:16; 11:28; 15:16, 19, 20; 16:25; I Cor. 4:15; 9:12, 14, 16, 18, 23; 15:1; 2 Cor. 2:12; 4:3; 8:18; 9:13; 10:14; 11:4, 7; Gal. 1:6, 8, 9, 11; 2:2, 5, 7, 14; 3:8; 4:13; Eph. 1:13; 3:6; 6:15, 19; Phil. 1:5, 12, 16, 27; 2:22; 4:3, 15; Col. 1:5; 1 Th. 1:5; 2:4, 8, 9; 3:2; 2 Th. 1:8; 2:14; 1 Tim. 1:11; 2 Tim. 1:8; Plm. 13; 1 Pet. 1:12; 4:6, 7; Rev. 5:6, 8, 12, 13; 6:1; 7:9, 10, 17; 13:8; 14:1, 4, 4, 6; 15:3; 17:14; 19:7, 9; 21:9, 14, 22, 23, 27; 22:1, 3

[6] Christ as an offering: Rom. 8:3; Eph. 5:2; Heb. 7:27; 9:25, 28; 10:10, 12, 14; as delivered up for us: Rom. 4:25; 8:32; as suffering for us: Rom. 8:17; 2 Cor. 1:5; Heb. 2:10, 18; 5:8; 9:26; 1 Pet. 1:11; 4:1, 13; 5:1; as a propitiation for our sins: Heb. 2:17; 1 Jn. 2:2; 4:10; as purchasing us: 1 Cor. 6:20; 2 Pet. 2:1; as a sacrifice: 1 Cor. 5:7; as having His body broken for us: 1 Cor. 11:24; as becoming sin for us: 2 Cor. 5:21; as becoming a curse for us: Gal. 3:13; as coming to save sinners: 1 Tim. 1:15; as ransoming us: 1 Tim. 2:6; as giving Himself: Gal. 1:4; Eph. 5:25; Tit. 2:14; as taking away sins: 1 Jn. 3:5; as laying down His life: 1 Jn. 3:16; as sent to be the Savior: 1 Jn. 4:14; as pierced for us; Rev. 1:7; as making purification for our sins: Heb. 1:3.

compare our preaching and teaching with that of the apostles. How many of us could claim that in our sermons one out of every thirteen sentences makes reference in some way to Jesus' death on the cross?

The Central Theme

Beyond this, as Smeaton observed, there is hardly a topic contained in the epistles that is not in some way connected to the doctrine of Christ's atoning sacrifice on the cross. How would it be possible to preach properly on the subjects of righteousness, justification, reconciliation, sanctification, redemption, forgiveness, sonship, faith, sin, peace with God, the new birth, our future resurrection, the Lord's Supper, baptism, future judgment, heaven, hell, the rapture of the church, the new covenant, God's grace, love, mercy, justice, holiness, in-Christ realities, Christ's ministry as our High Priest and Advocate, victory over sin, or Satan's defeat, without mention of Jesus' death on the cross?

Furthermore, how could we properly teach about such subjects as the love of the brethren, our obligation to forgive others, marriage, humility, or enduring hardship and persecution, without relating them, as did the apostles, to Jesus' great example on the cross?[7]

In light of the above facts, it is certainly an indictment upon our preaching when we feel we must make a choice between *either* evangelistic preaching *or* feeding the Christians on Sunday mornings. There are very few topics contained in the New Testament epistles that are not built upon the foundation of Christ's sacrificial death; thus, it should always be an easy matter to naturally blend the "word of the cross" into our sermons.

If a preacher is finding it hard to include Jesus' vicarious death naturally into his sermons then he ought to re-examine what he is preaching. Quite possibly, either he is teaching something that none of the apostles would be caught teaching, or he is presenting something in a way that the apostles would never have presented it.

[7] Christ's death as our example in loving the brethren: Rom. 14:15; 15:1-3; 1 Jn. 4:10-11; in forgiving others: Eph. 4:32; Col. 3:12-13; Matt. 18:21-35; in marriage: Eph. 5:22-33; in humility: Phil. 2:5-8; in enduring hardship and persecution: Heb. 12:3; 1 Pet. 2:21-23.

Keeping Our Message Balanced

Modern American Christianity offers, through its many sincere teachers and counselors, unlimited seminars on numerous topics. While many of these teachings are related to the Bible, I have found they are often mixed with a dose of psychology and human conjecture.

Presently it seems that marriage seminars are in vogue. I thank God for the marriages that have been helped and healed by this means, but can you imagine the Apostle Paul (or any of the apostles) visiting a local church to host a four-day marriage seminar? Can you imagine the listing of his sermon topics, such as "How to Understand Your Mate," and "How to Handle Disputes About Finances," and "How to Meet the Psychological Needs of Your Wife"?

For those who know the New Testament, the thought of such a scene is laughable. Of course, we know that Paul certainly did instruct his converts concerning marriage, and his counsel was short, to the point, and profound. He told husbands to love their wives just as Christ loved the church and gave Himself up for her, and he told wives to submit to their husbands as the church is subject to Christ.

Paul's instructions are only understandable to those who understand the cross. Following the inspiration and example of the cross, those who believe in the message of the cross have God-glorifying marriages. If Christian husbands and wives would obey Paul's simple instructions, their marital problems would end.

Is it possible that the fundamental reason why marriage seminars are so necessary in the church today is because so few Christians have a true revelation of the cross of Jesus Christ? *Once the cross has truly captured one's heart, he sees and treats others differently, including his mate.* That man or woman you are married to is one for whom Christ died.

Of course I'm not saying that we should no longer teach about Christian marriage. But I am saying that all our teaching should be Christ-centered and, thus, cross-centered. Those of us who call ourselves ministers would be wise to follow Paul's admonition to Timothy: "Preach the word" (2 Tim 4:2). If we do, our preaching will be anointed by God. If we don't, our preaching won't be anointed. It may be entertaining, it may be enlightening, it may even be somewhat helpful, but it won't be anointed.

I could go much further with an analysis of many modern trends in the church, but I'm afraid that perhaps the wrath of a sizeable portion of evangelical Christianity would fall upon me. But may I say, with as much restraint as possible, that those of us who teach and instruct others in Christ's body need to ask ourselves, "Where in Scripture can I find an apostolic precedent for what I preach and teach?" When the teaching in the church becomes nothing more than a series of self-help and success-motivation seminars sanctified by a few out-of-context scriptures, something is definitely wrong.

Have you ever wondered why the early Christians displayed such a high level of commitment when compared to modern believers? Peter, James, and John did not have the book of Acts to preach from in order to motivate their flock to act like the people of the book of Acts (as we often try to do)!

They had a simple message of One who died for our sins, which effected a change in those who believed it. They were truly born-again—not just "converted," not just "Christian hobbyists." That message motivated people to repent of their sins and live for the One who died for them. That message was not man-centered but cross-centered and Christ-centered.

Are we emphasizing what the New Testament emphasizes? Is our message as balanced as the New Testament?

Why Preach the Cross?

Although examining every reference to Christ's atoning death in the epistles would be profitable, it would require a lengthy commentary far beyond the scope of this book. Just a preliminary study of primary references would necessitate a perusal of 212 verses (listed in footnotes number 3, 5 and 6) and would not include the numerous indirect and related references to the cross. Therefore, our study will be limited to a few passages from the writings of the Apostle Paul.

In this chapter, we will examine specific passages in 1 Corinthians, Galatians, and finally Romans. In particular, we will be investigating the centrality of the cross in Paul's preaching and examine his explanation of how Christ's death saves us. In subsequent chapters we will examine scriptures that concern themselves with the accomplishments and implications of the cross.

No other epistle so clearly discloses the centrality of the cross as does Paul's letter to the Corinthians. Although I've previously mentioned the following verses, they are worthy of a second examination:

> For Christ did not send me to baptize, but to preach the gospel, not in cleverness of speech, that the *cross of Christ* should not be made void. For the *word of the cross* is to those who are perishing foolishness, but to us who are being saved it is the power of God (1 Cor. 1:17-18; italics mine).

Quite obviously, according to Paul's statement, "the gospel" and "the word of the cross" are synonymous terms. Paul told us that "the word of the cross" is *the power of God* to us who are being saved. He used the identical expression in His letter to the Romans, calling "the gospel" *the power of God* for salvation (Rom. 1:16). The gospel *is* "the word of the cross." *If the cross has not been mentioned, the gospel has not been preached.*

Because the word of the cross is the power of God, Paul told us that he was careful to let nothing diminish its simple message; thus he resisted the temptation to use "cleverness of speech," lest the "cross of Christ should be made void."

How we need to recapture his viewpoint today! Too often, the cross of Christ is voided by our pathetic attempts to make the gospel more appetizing to the world. Not convinced that the cross can be left to stand as it is, we obscure it behind the dust-clouds of human reasoning. Or we attempt to smooth its roughness through our eloquent sermons and clever methods of evangelism, while, in reality, we insult it. Once smoothed, we may refinish it, trying to make it "relevant" by presenting the cross as a panacea for psychological ills or a way to the good life. In every case, the cross is being voided.

No Compromise

Just a few verses later, Paul again affirmed the cross was central to his message:

> For indeed Jews ask for signs, and Greeks search for wisdom; *but we preach Christ crucified,* to Jews a stumbling block, and to Gentiles foolishness....And when I came to you, brethren, I did not come with superiority of speech or of wisdom, proclaiming to you the testimony of God. For *I determined to know nothing among except Jesus Christ, and Him crucified.* (1 Cor. 1:22-23; 2:1-2; italics mine).

Although Paul was careful to avoid offending his audiences because of cultural peculiarities, he never compromised his message for the sake of gaining more converts. We must see that the gospel does not need to be made relevant—*it already is relevant*—because it provides the answer to humanity's greatest need: the forgiveness of sins.

Some have reasoned, "So many people want to get rich, so let's tell them that if they accept Jesus, God will prosper them financially. That will attract them."

Rather than telling the unsaved that greed is one of the sins that will send them to hell, some preachers actually fuel their listeners' greed by means of a "gospel"! I certainly agree that God wants His children to prosper, but that is not the gospel we are to take to the world. The gospel calls people to repent of greed (as well as other sins) because they cannot serve God and money, as Jesus told us.

Later in his letter to the Corinthians, Paul's gospel is unveiled further. He did not preach just the historical fact of Christ's death but also its significance. He preached that Christ died for our sins:

> Now I make known to you, brethren, *the gospel which I preached* to you, which also you received, in which also you stand, by which also you are saved, if you hold fast the word I preached to you....For I delivered to you as of *first importance* what I also received, *that Christ died for our sins* according to the Scriptures, and that He was buried, and that He was raised on the third day according to the Scriptures, and that He appeared to Cephas, then to the twelve (1 Cor. 15:1-5; italics mine).

When Paul first preached the gospel to the Corinthians, he told them that Jesus had died as their substitute, suffering God's wrath for their sins according to the Old Testament predictions. No doubt the 53rd chapter of Isaiah was a well-used text.

The Authentic Gospel

Paul did not reserve these truths solely for Corinthian ears—it was his consistent message. He wrote to the Galatians:

> *I have been crucified with Christ;* and it is no longer I who live, but Christ lives in me; and the life which I now live in the flesh I live by faith in the Son God, *who loved me and delivered Himself up for me.* I do not nullify the grace of God; for if righteousness comes through the Law, then Christ died needlessly. You foolish Galatians, who has bewitched you, before whose eyes *Jesus Christ was publicly portrayed as crucified?* (Gal. 2:20 - 3:1; italics mine).

Paul's preaching of the gospel was so cross-centered that he could describe it as a public portrayal of Christ's crucifixion. Jesus was portrayed as one who "delivered Himself up for" us, and thus satisfied the claims of the law on our behalf. Thus, we have been crucified with Him since He was our substitute. Through His sacrifice, the gift of righteousness is offered to all. That is the good news.

In the book of Romans, we find the clearest exposition of the gospel offered in the epistles. In the lengthy introduction of the first chapter, where Paul used the words *the gospel* four times, he prepared his readers for an explanation of how Christ's death saves us. His explanation in the chapters that follow establishes a standard by which all gospel-preaching should be measured. The mark of the authentic gospel, as Paul stated in his introduction, is that it reveals "the righteousness of God":

> For I am not ashamed of the gospel, for it is the power of God for salvation to every one who believes, to the Jew first and also to the Greek. For in it *the righteousness of God* is revealed from faith to faith; as it is written, "But the righteous man shall live by faith" (Rom. 1:16-17; italics mine).

How is God's righteousness revealed in the gospel? Paul began to explain in his very next sentence:

> For the wrath of God is revealed from heaven against all
> ungodliness and unrighteousness of men, who suppress the
> truth in unrighteousness..." (Rom. 1:18).

Two fundamental concepts are introduced in this sentence:
humanity's unrighteousness and God's wrath against humanity's
unrighteousness. These two truths are axioms upon which the
gospel is built. *Without them, Christ's death is meaningless.*

Because God is righteous and all people are unrighteous, all
people deserve God's wrath. If God, the moral Judge of the
universe, did not inflict wrath upon unrighteousness, then He
Himself would be unrighteous. He *must* punish the guilty.

How could a loving God offer sinful humanity forgiveness—
when they deserved nothing other than His wrath—and at the same
time maintain His righteousness? It was, as Martin Luther described it, "a problem worthy of God," and one that was solved by
Jesus' death.

The authentic gospel reveals God's righteousness. God is
shown *righteously* offering all people forgiveness because His
wrath was poured out upon Jesus. God did not compromise His
righteousness; our sins were punished in Christ, and because of it,
God's righteousness can be imputed to us.

The authentic gospel will always reveal God's righteousness
because it proclaims that Jesus died for our sins, suffering as our
substitute. By His death, the gift of righteousness is freely offered
to all who will believe. Using this criteria we can discern what is
the true gospel and what is not. *A gospel that does not reveal God's
righteousness is not the gospel.*

For this reason, we should beware of any gospel that disregards
or neglects the foundational axioms of humanity's guilt and God's
wrath. Both truths have been attacked from various quarters, and
it will do us well to take a moment and shore up these twin pillars
of truth.

The Sinfulness of Humanity

One would think that humanity's sinfulness is a self-evident
fact against which none would argue. Yet it has been questioned,

not only by those outside the church, but even by some within it. The very fact that some argue against it, however, only serves to undergird its veracity; only a *proud* sinner would dream that he is not a sinner!

Is humanity sinful? That question is best answered with a few other questions: Why is there a need for laws in every society? Why are there courts in session and a backlog of people waiting for trials? Why are the jails overcrowded? Why do the yellow pages contain such long listings of lawyers? Why do we need police? Why do we need an army? Why must we lock our doors?

Why must we purchase tickets for a baseball game rather than abide by an honor system? Why are business contracts necessary? Why must departments stores hire detectives? Why do our employers withhold taxes from our paychecks? Why must we produce identification when we write out checks? Why do we have racial violence, a fifty-percent divorce rate, rampant use of illegal drugs, a billion-dollar pornography industry? All of these questions indict us as transgressors of God's moral law.

In his letter to the Romans, Paul lays a foundation for the good news of Jesus' sacrifice by repeatedly asserting humanity's guilt before God. Here is a sample:

> ...being filled with all unrighteousness, wickedness, greed, malice; full of envy, murder, strife, deceit, malice; they are gossips, slanderers, haters of God, insolent, arrogant, boastful, inventors of evil, disobedient to parents, without understanding, untrustworthy, unloving, unmerciful... (Rom. 1:29-31).

Over the past few years, the contemporary self-esteem psychology has infiltrated the church, and we now hear some preachers telling us that man's greatest problem is that he doesn't love himself as he should. He is not a sinner—he just has a poor self-image. But if he will open his heart to God, who truly loves him for what he is, then his damaged self-esteem can be repaired and he'll discover true fulfilment.

But this is not what the Bible teaches or the gospel reveals. God does love everyone, but God loves humans *in spite* of what they do.

Unregenerate man has no real basis for possessing a good self-image. Man *feels* guilty because man *is* guilty! His conduct should shame him as his God-given conscience condemns him.

Only one who has believed in Jesus and been born-again has any true basis for a good self-image. But his view of himself should rest solely on his worth through the cross by which he has been reconciled to God. There is no room for pride in the Christian—all his worth stems from God. For that reason alone may we love ourselves.

Guilty or Not Guilty?

Not only does Paul affirm humanity's sinfulness, but he also declares that every person knows full well he is guilty and, therefore, without excuse. Guilt is an acquaintance universally known by the human race because God has given each person a conscience endorsing His moral law. Our conscience testifies that we will one day give account of ourselves before God:

> For when the Gentiles who do not have the [Mosaic] Law do instinctively the things of the Law, these, not having the Law, are a law to themselves, in that they show the work of the Law written in their hearts, their conscience bearing witness, and their thoughts alternately accusing or else defending them, on the day when, according to my gospel, God will judge the secrets of men through Christ Jesus (Rom. 2:14-16).

Paul also contended that we all stand self-condemned because all of us have condemned others for doing what we ourselves have done:

> Therefore you are without excuse, every man of you who passes judgment, for in that you judge another, you condemn yourself; for you who judge practice the same things. And we know that the judgment of God rightly falls upon those who practice such things. And do you suppose this, O man, when you pass judgment upon those who practice such things and do the same yourself, that you will escape the judgment of God? (Rom. 2:1-3).

The sins we commit against others can all be placed under one category: selfishness. When we criticize others for their selfishness we are openly testifying before the court of heaven that we know what is right and what is wrong. And by our judgments of others, we condemn ourselves because we are just as guilty as those we condemn.

The greatest single affirmation of humanity's sinfulness is Jesus' death itself. Martyn Lloyd-Jones wrote:

> The cross thus proclaims the holiness of God, the heinousness of sin, the terrible problem of sin, the terrible seriousness of man's rebellion against God."[8]

If humanity is not sinful, Jesus would not have needed to suffer on our behalf. The Scripture says He "bore our sins in His body on the cross" (1 Pet. 2:24) and was thus punished in our stead. This is why the doctrine of humanity's sinfulness is so vital to the gospel.

If humanity is not sinful, then Christ's death was meaningless for two reasons. First, if people are not sinful, they don't need to be saved; they need not fear God's wrath. And second, if people are not sinful, then our sins were not laid on Jesus because there were none to lay upon Him.

The true gospel cannot be preached without mention of humanity's sin because the gospel offers people forgiveness of sins. A.W. Tozer expressed this truth in his book, *The Knowledge of the Holy*:

> When the man's laboring conscience tells him that he...has from childhood been guilty of foul revolt against the Majesty in heavens, the inner pressure of self-accusation may become too heavy to bear. The gospel can lift this destroying burden from the mind...*But unless the weight of the burden is felt the gospel can mean nothing to the man*...(italics mine).[9]

Does God Get Angry?

Even more undermined than humanity's sinfulness is the doctrine of God's wrath, which is equally foundational to the biblical gospel.

[8] Martyn Lloyd-Jones, *The Cross*, p. 159.

[9] A.W. Tozer, *The Knowledge of the Holy*, p. 11, italics mine.

Some have looked at wrath as an attribute unbefitting of God, but their error has been in equating God's wrath with human wrath. God does not become angry as people do. As the apostle James wrote, "the anger of man does not achieve the righteousness of God" (Jas. 1:20). God's anger is always perfect in righteousness. We should never imagine Him as an impetuous dictator overcome by some fit of rage. J.I. Packer has said it well:

> God's wrath in the Bible is never the capricious, self-indulgent, irritable, morally ignoble thing that human anger often is. It is, instead, a right and necessary reaction to objective moral evil. God is only angry where anger is called for. Even among men, there is such a thing as *righteous* indignation, though it is, perhaps, rarely found. But all of God's indignation is righteous. Would a God who took as much pleasure in evil as He did good be a good God? Would a God who did not react adversely to evil in His world be morally perfect? Surely not.[10]

The typical shallow argument against God's wrath is that He is love, and "surely a loving God would never punish anyone." But as Packer states, a morally perfect being cannot look on evil and good with the same response.

What would we think of a parent who, under the guise of love, never punished his son who repeatedly harms his other son? The parent's love demands that he love them equally, and thus he must treat them with fairness.

Love demands that wrongdoing be punished. Because God is perfect love, He acts with perfect justice, favoring no person above another. If He did not react against the selfish deeds of people, He would not be perfect in love. *Therefore, if God is love, then He must also be wrathful.*

God's wrath is hardly an obscure subject in the Bible. In fact, there are approximately 168 direct references where the word *wrath* is used in Scripture.

Is God's wrath only an Old Testament concept, as some have claimed? No, the New Testament comprises 23% of the Bible and

[10] J.I. Packer, *Knowing God*, p. 136.

claims 20% of the direct references to God's wrath.

If we add direct references to God's *anger*, *fury*, and *indignation*, our total climbs to at least 465 Bible references. And we still aren't taking into account the passages that convey God's anger and wrath without specifically calling it such, or the many references concerning future punishment and hell, many of which fell directly from the lips of Jesus. If God is not a God of wrath, then we should throw our Bibles out with the garbage.

Opening the Door to God's Wrath

One of the most subtle assaults on God's wrath is the idea swallowed by many charismatic Christians that "God doesn't punish anyone—they just open the door to the devil." The whole concept is designed to defend God's loving character, but it actually defames His character when compared to biblical revelation. It is comparable to the idea held by those liberal theologians who try to explain God's wrath as only the natural consequences for wrongdoing, consequences in which God is not personally involved.

Although it is certainly true that God may send His wrath upon the wicked by permitting Satan to afflict them,[11] God is still very much involved; Satan is only acting by His permission. God's wrath is not something that operates independently of His being; again and again He refers to it as "My wrath" and "My anger."[12]

If God is not involved in bringing wrath on wrongdoing and people are only "opening the door to Satan," then Satan has become God. If Satan is the sole punisher of wrongdoing, then God has become Satan, immoral and unjust.

The truth is that people open the door to *God's wrath* through sin. God's wrath *may* be discharged by permitting Satan to afflict wrongdoers although it can come directly from God Himself (as the Bible so clearly indicates).[13]

[11] See Judg. 9:22-24; 1 Sam. 16:14-23; Mal. 3:8-11; Mt. 18:21-35; 1 Cor. 5:1-5.

[12] For a thorough treatment of this subject, see Leon Morris' *The Apostolic Preaching of the Cross*, pp. 177-84

[13] For New Testament examples of God's wrath being administered by God Himself, see Lk. 12:4-5; Acts 12:23; 13:11; 1 Cor. 3:17; Jas. 4:12; Rev. 2:21-23; 22:18-19. The Old Testament has too many examples to list.

Why is the doctrine of God's wrath so vital? Because if God is not a God of wrath, then, once again, Christ's death is meaningless for two reasons.

First, if there is no such thing as God's wrath, then people have no reason to be concerned. There is no need to be saved because there is nothing from which to be saved. God will never punish anyone; there is no hell to fear.

And second, if God's wrath doesn't exist, then Jesus didn't suffer God's wrath on the cross, He just died as a martyr. That means His death has no ability to save anyone because He didn't die in our place.

As Paul explained the gospel in the first chapters of his Roman epistle, God's wrath is a predominant theme, and no wonder. He asserted that God's wrath is not only something people will experience *some day*, but it is a *present* reality. God's wrath is not just *going to be* revealed; Paul stated that it *is being* revealed.

Of course, those who have read the Old Testament know that many of the wars, tragedies, and calamities of human history were a result of God's sovereign judgment upon evildoers. But Paul went even further, stating three times in the first chapter that God is actively judging people at present by "turning them over" to practice increasing decadence along with its consequent suffering.

Putting God's Kindness in Perspective

In the second chapter of Romans, Paul's takes an even stronger stand for God's wrath:

> And we know that the *judgment of God* rightly falls upon those who practice such things. And do you suppose this, O man, when you pass judgment upon those who practice such things and do the same yourself, that you will escape *the judgment of God?* [Of course, the thought is preposterous.] Or do you think lightly of the riches of His kindness and forbearance and patience, not knowing that the kindness of God leads you to repentance? But because of your stubbornness and unrepentant heart you are storing up *wrath* for yourself in the day of *wrath* and revelation of the righteous judgment of God, who will render to every man according

to his deeds: to those who by perseverance in doing good seek for glory and honor and immortality, eternal life; but to those who are selfishly ambitious and do not obey the truth, but obey unrighteousness, *wrath* and *indignation*. There will be *tribulation* and *distress* for every soul of man who does evil..." (Rom. 2:2-9; italics mine).

It is incredible that some have taken Paul's statement, "the kindness of God leads you to repentance," as a proof that we should never mention God's wrath, hell, or judgment when preaching the gospel. "Just tell them about God's love," they say, "because it's the kindness of God that leads people to repentance."

But that very statement ("the kindness of God.") is found nested among several other sentences that again and again declare God's wrath and the terrible fate that awaits the unrepentant! Why? *Because God's kindness is best seen in the light of His holiness, wrath, and judgment*. God's kindness is revealed by His sending Jesus to suffer His wrath in our stead, so that we could escape His wrath. *Truly, the greater revelation one gains of humanity's sinfulness and God's wrath, the greater revelation one gains of God's amazing love displayed in Christ*.

Also notice that God's kindness is said to lead people to *repentance*. When people respond to the *true* gospel, they are *naturally* led to repent because they understand that their sins are what separate them from God. Then they comprehend *why* Jesus suffered and died.

But just telling people that God is kind provides no stimulus to repentance. People must hear the "word of the cross," which means they will hear about humanity's sin, God's wrath, and Jesus the sin-bearer. If their hearts are soft, they'll repent and receive Jesus as Savior.

Safe from God's Wrath

After using fifty-nine sentences to lay a foundation of two truths—namely *humanity's guilt* and *God's holy wrath*—Paul then arrives at the climax of his gospel. In Romans 3:21-28, he explains how Jesus saves us from God's wrath. Let's examine this passage, piece by piece:

But now apart from the Law *the righteousness of God* has

been manifested... (Rom. 3:21a; italics mine).

Paul had previously stated that the gospel reveals God's righteousness. Here we read that God's righteousness is manifested by something other than the Law. Of course, he must be speaking of the gospel of Christ's substitutionary death. Through its many commandments and promised punishments, the Law revealed that God is righteous. But Christ's death also reveals it because Jesus was being punished for sins—our sins.

I might add that if Jesus was *not* crucified for our sins, then His death would prove that God is *unrighteous*, due to the fact that Jesus was an innocent man.

Paul went on to write that God's righteousness was

> ...witnessed by the Law and the Prophets, even the righteousness of God through faith in Jesus Christ for all those who believe; for there is no distinction; for all have sinned and fall short of the glory of God, being justified as a gift by His grace... (Rom. 3:21b-24a).

Just as our sins were imputed to Christ, God's righteousness is imputed to us once we believe the gospel. It comes through Jesus as a gift of God's grace, that is, His undeserved favor.

> ...through the redemption which is in Christ Jesus, whom God displayed publicly as a propitiation in His blood through faith (Rom. 3:24b-25a).

The word *propitiate* means "to appease or to turn away anger." Paul points out that when Jesus was shedding His blood on the cross, God was publicly displaying Him as the One who would avert God's anger against us.

> *This was* to demonstrate His righteousness, because in the forbearance of God He passed over sins previously committed; for the demonstration, *I say,* of His righteousness at the present time, that He might be just [righteous] and the justifier [the One who makes people righteous] of the one who has faith in Jesus (Rom 25b-26; italics are NASB).

As Paul stated in his introduction and here explained, the gospel of Jesus' death reveals God's righteousness.

Leon Morris elucidates this passage:

> The fact that God had not always punished sin with full severity in the past, but had "passed over" such sin, gave rise to the danger that He might not appear to men to be completely righteous. But now, in the cross, He has for ever removed that danger. He has shown Himself to be completely righteous.[14]

Finally we read verses 27-28:

> Where then is boasting? It is excluded. By what kind of law? Of works? No, but by a law of faith. For we maintain that a man is justified by faith apart from the works of the Law (Rom. 3:27-28).

The message of Christ's substitutionary death eradicates the idea that our good works could save us. In fact, His death reveals the magnitude of our debt of sin. If it were possible for us to be saved by works, then there would have been no need for the Son of God to suffer and die. Righteousness cannot be earned—it is offered freely on the basis of Jesus' sacrifice. He earned it for us.

In Roman's chapter 5, Paul listed the primary blessing that we receive because of Jesus' death—escape from God's wrath:

> But God demonstrates His own love toward us, in that while we were yet sinners, Christ died for us. Much more then, having now been justified by His blood, we shall be saved from the wrath of God through Him (Rom. 5:8-9).

It would be unjust for God to punish the same sin twice. Therefore, because Christ was punished, those of us who have believed the gospel need not fear God's wrath. Praise God!

Two Commonly Asked Questions

In reference to the above-quoted scripture and others like it, a question often arises: How can Christ's *blood* be said to save us? Does Paul mean that we are saved by Jesus' red and white blood cells, His platelets, glucose, amino acids, carbon dioxide, urea, and plasma? No. Leon Morris in his book, *The Apostolic Preaching of*

---

[14] Leon Morris, *The Apostolic Preaching of the Cross*, p. 278.

the Cross, has very thoroughly and convincingly proven that the word "blood"—as it is most often used in Scripture—simply refers to violent death.[15]

We say that Christ's blood saves us just as we might say that the cross saves us. Obviously two logs are not what saves us, but it is what happened upon those beams. J. Behm wrote, "Like the cross...the 'blood of Christ' is simply another and even more graphic phrase for the death of Christ in its soteriological [salvation] significance."[16]

Another commonly asked question is: How could Jesus' brief suffering on the cross serve as payment for people who were condemned to suffer eternally in hell?

The answer lies in the fact of *who* did the suffering. It wasn't an ordinary man hanging on the cross—it was God. Whether we fully understand it or not, in the court of heaven, Jesus' suffering was declared sufficient to atone for the sins of humanity. Of that, we can be sure.

An illustration, although perhaps a poor one, may be helpful. Imagine that your German Shepherd attacks and kills your neighbor's poodle. For justice to be done, you would be required to pay the man for the loss of his dog.

If he demands absolute justice, then he might ask that your dog be killed so that you would suffer just as he has. In that case, not only would you suffer for the irresponsibility of letting your German Shepherd loose, but your dog would also suffer, reaping exactly what he had sown.

But imagine your neighbor, rather than demanding your dog's death, demands *your* death! You would certainly object, knowing that you have infinitely more value than your neighbor's poodle! Even if your German Shepherd killed every other dog in your city, it would still not require your execution![17]

---

[15] See Leon Morris, *The Apostolic Preaching of the Cross,* pp. 112-26.

[16] G. Kittel (ed.), *Theological Dictionary of the New Testament* Vol. 1, p. 174.

[17] The reason this illustration is imperfect is because dogs are not held morally responsible for their actions, as men are. God is not responsible for the immoral actions of man, as the owner is responsible for his dog's misconduct. However, God the Son voluntarily took the liability for man's sin, suffering on behalf of lesser persons.

Because it was the divine Son of God who suffered, His sufferings had infinite value, certainly sufficient to atone for the sins of humanity.

We can *speculate* that *if* God could have found one sinless human being who would have been willing to die as a substitute, then that substitute *would* have had to spend an eternity in hell. Such suffering, however, would have only been sufficient to atone for *one* other human being. But the Person who suffered on the cross for us had infinitely greater value than all humans combined, as they are just a creation, and He is their Creator.

Although we know Jesus' suffering was of a short duration (relative to eternity), we really have no comprehension as to the degree He actually suffered. It's impossible for us to imagine the agony Jesus endured when God's full cup of wrath was poured out on Him. But at the end of it all, God saw "the anguish of His soul" as Isaiah said,[18] and was satisfied. Justice had been meted out to the human race in the person of the Son of God.

[18] Is. 53:11

NINE

The Profuse Blessings
of the Cross

The New Testament authors, in explaining the gospel, used various terms to describe the benefits that are ours as a result of Christ's sacrificial death. Each one underscores some blessing that the atonement brings, and together they give us a complete picture of what Christ accomplished for us. The biblical terms we will briefly survey are *propitiation, justification, reconciliation, redemption,* and, finally, *salvation.*

Propitiation: Turning Away God's Wrath

Those who have difficulty believing that God is wrathful have great difficulty with *propitiation* because propitiate means "to turn away wrath." Although the word is found only four times in the New Testament, it succinctly embodies a truth often repeated in Scripture. This truth brings us directly to the heart of the gospel: Jesus' death turned away God's wrath against us.

If hell is a real place where people dwell eternally after death, and if Jesus' death saves believers from that place, then propitiation is the best word to describe the preeminent accomplishment of the cross. Jesus "delivers us from the wrath to come" (1 Thes. 1:10).

In the previous chapter we learned that God is indeed a God who cannot wink at disobedience, but who is, as the Bible states, "a God who has indignation every day" (Ps. 7:11). If He is a "righteous judge" as the Bible says He is, then His anger should not surprise us. If God remained passive while witnessing the selfish acts of humanity, then He would be unjust. Furthermore, He would be a hypocrite for He has commanded us to act always with fairness.

Those proponents of the all-loving, never-angered God should read the Apostle John's first letter. There he writes that God's love was *demonstrated* by Jesus' act of propitiating God's wrath:

> In this is love, not that we loved God, but that He loved us and sent His Son to be the *propitiation* for our sins (1 Jn. 4:10; italics mine).

God has proven His love by sending His own Son to appease His wrath against us. If we are going to discard the concept of propitiation, we must also discard God's love. In fact, we must reject the very gospel itself.

Earlier in his first epistle, John wrote,

> ...and He Himself is the *propitiation* for our sins; and not for ours only, but also for those of the whole world (1 Jn. 2:2; italics mine).

(John says plainly that Jesus' saving act was not only the propitiation for the sins of believers but also for unbelievers. Of course, each unbeliever must repent and believe the gospel before Christ's saving work becomes effectual in his life.)

Through the offering of Christ, God has been propitiated. His anger against us has been turned away. But as we consider the meaning of propitiation, it is important that we not equate the crude pagan notions of propitiation with that of biblical Christianity. The two are worlds apart.

First of all, in pagan religions, the worshiper falls prey to the wrath of his god for arbitrary, often unpredictable and whimsical reasons. But God's anger is always predictable because it is only aroused by sin. His anger is always perfectly righteous.

Second, the pagan propitiates his angry god by means of some sacrifice *he himself* offers. The Bible teaches us that we could never hope to pacify God's wrath by any effort or sacrifice of our own. God has appeased Himself by the offering of a sacrifice of infinite value, His very own Son who merited salvation for us.

This puts Christian propitiation on an infinitely higher plane than pagan religion's meager offerings. It was not some incense, some coins, or some animal that was placed on an altar—it was God Himself who was the sacrifice.

Leon Morris has summed up these two points nicely:

> The Bible writers have nothing to do with pagan conceptions of a capricious and vindictive deity, inflicting arbitrary punishments on offending worshippers, who then must bribe him back to a good mood by the appropriate offerings.[1]

Also, we must not think that Jesus was the "nice guy" who laid down his life to appease "the mean guy." It was "God in Christ" who gave Himself for our sins. As Jesus Himself declared, He was and is one with the Father (see Jn 10:30, 38; 17:11, 21-22).

God loved us and propitiated His own wrath by giving Himself. Jesus' sacrifice is not what made God love us; He already loved us, which is why He gave His Son.

Justification: Declared Innocent

Justification is a legal term signifying a verdict of acquittal. One who is justified is declared innocent or righteous. In fact, the New Testament words translated *justified*, *justification*, *righteous*, and *righteousness* are all derived from the same root word in the original Greek language. If you are justified, or possess justification, then you are righteous and possess righteousness. So as we study justification, we should also include those scriptures which refer to the *righteousness* we possess through Christ.

Being justified implies more than just being forgiven. When a person is justified in court, it means he is declared innocent of all charges against him.

In Christ, we are found "not guilty"! And thus *God will treat us as if we've never sinned*. God no longer views us as guilt-stained

[1] Leon Morris, *The Apostolic Preaching of the Cross*, p. 148.

sinners; nor does He view us as pardoned criminals; *He views us as never having been guilty!*

Even more incredible, righteousness is not something that is earned; the New Testament calls it a gift from God. I realize this may sound too good to be true, but it *is* true. Just as our sin was imputed to Christ, so His righteousness has been imputed to us:

> He [God] made Him [Jesus] who knew no sin *to be* sin on our behalf, that we might become the righteousness of God in Him (2 Cor. 5:21; italics NASB).

Christ was and is perfect in righteousness. He never sinned, and now His righteousness is ours! God now treats us as if we had never sinned!

If you are a Christian, you'll never have a more righteous standing with God than you do now. The above scripture said we have become God's own righteousness. You can't become more righteous than that!

The benefits of being justified are manifold. Being justified means we not only have the peace *of* God—we have peace *with* God and have no reason to fear His wrath:

> Therefore having been *justified* by faith, we have peace with God through our Lord Jesus Christ....Much more then, having now been *justified* by His blood, we shall be saved from the wrath of God through Him (Rom. 5:1, 9; italics mine).

Being justified assures us that we will one day be glorified with Christ and that we need never fear being condemned:

> ...and whom He called, these He also *justified;* and whom He *justified,* these He also glorified. What then shall we say to these things? If God is for us, who is against us? He who did not spare His own Son, but delivered Him up for us all, how will He not also with Him freely give us all things? Who will bring a charge against God's elect? God is the one who *justifies;* who is the one who condemns? (Rom. 8:30b-34a; italics mine).

Being justified means that we have access to God and can

confidently make our requests before Him, knowing that "the effective prayer of a *righteous* man can accomplish much" (Jas. 5:16; italics mine).

No doubt the greatest hindrance to faith in our prayers is the consciousness that we have sinned. This is why Jesus instructed us to pray in His name.

The phrase "in Jesus' name" was not given to the church to use as a lucky rabbit's foot. It is a reminder to us that we have access to God through Jesus, and that our only right of request is what He has done for us. It can be truly said that when we pray according to God's revealed will, we have just as much right to expect our prayers to be answered as if we were Jesus Himself praying. We possess His righteousness!

Reconciliation: Enemies Become Friends

Before our new birth, we were at enmity with God and He was at enmity with us. Of course, He has always loved us, but our sins separated us from Him.

Some wonder how God could love us and yet at the same time be our enemy. But the answer is simply that *God loves His enemies.* Christians should understand this because we are commanded to love *our* enemies by following God's example. This doesn't mean that God expects us to say of our enemies, "They are really wonderful people." It means that we are to show them mercy, do good to them even when they don't deserve it, and desire the best for them. They may hate us, and we may hate what they do, but we should love them.

Obviously, this kind of love is of a different realm than the selfish, feeling-oriented emotion that the world calls love. God's love transcends feelings and is a willful decision to treat undeserving people with kindness.

The good news of the gospel is that Jesus' saving act on the cross has provided the means of our reconciliation with God. We are no longer enemies—but friends—because Jesus bore the penalty of the law that condemned us, satisfying the claims of divine justice.

The references to our reconciliation in the epistles are not nearly as numerous as those to our justification (or being made righteous).

127

There are five passages, and I can't resist showing four of them to you. I begin with a few verses from Romans:

> For if while we were enemies, we were *reconciled* to God through the death of His Son, much more, having been *reconciled*, we shall be saved by His life. And not only this, but we also exult in God through our Lord Jesus Christ, through whom we have now received the *reconciliation* (Rom. 5:10-11; italics mine).

We note that although God has reconciled the world to Himself, it remains for each individual to receive his reconciliation. Notice, too, that it was *Christ's death* that effected our reconciliation, not any supposed sufferings in hell.

> Now all these things are from God, who *reconciled* us to Himself through Christ, and gave us the ministry of *reconciliation*, namely, that God was in Christ *reconciling* the world to Himself, not counting their trespasses against them, and He has committed to us the word of *reconciliation*. Therefore, we are ambassadors for Christ, as though God were entreating through us; we beg you on behalf of Christ, be *reconciled* to God. He made Him who knew no sin to be sin on our behalf, that we might become the righteousness of God in Him (2 Cor. 5:18-21; italics mine).

All of us, like Paul, have been given a ministry of reconciliation. We can tell the world that God was in Christ and that He has reconciled the world to Himself through Jesus, who bore their sins on the cross. Now, through us, He is entreating them to be reconciled to God and receive forgiveness of their sins.

> But now in Christ Jesus you [Gentiles] who formerly were far off have been brought near by the blood of Christ. For He Himself is our peace, who made both *groups into* one [Jews and Gentiles], and broke down the barrier of the dividing wall, by abolishing in His flesh the enmity, *which is* the Law of commandments *contained* in ordinances, that in Himself He might make the two into one new man, thus establishing peace, and might *reconcile* them both in one body to God through the cross, by it having put to death the enmity....for

through Him we both have our access in one Spirit to the Father (Eph. 2:13-18; italics mine on the word "reconcile").

Here it is affirmed that both Jews and Gentiles were under the penal sentence of the law they had broken, but that through the cross the enmity of the law has been abolished. This includes the moral law that all people have broken, and the Mosaic Law which was only given to and broken by the Jews. Now we have peace with God because our sentence has been executed upon Christ, and in Him Jews and Gentiles have peace with each other.

> For it was the Father's good pleasure for all the fulness to dwell in Him, and through Him to *reconcile* all things to Himself, having made peace through the blood of His cross....And although you were formerly alienated and hostile in mind, engaged in evil deeds, yet He has now *reconciled* you in His fleshly body through death, in order to present you before Him holy and blameless and beyond reproach—if indeed you continue in the faith firmly established and steadfast, and not moved away from the hope of the gospel... (Col. 1:19-23a; italics mine).

Again it's clear that we were reconciled in Christ's *fleshly body through death* and not by any supposed sufferings He experienced in hell.

As a result, we are now holy and blameless and beyond reproach if we continue to believe the gospel. Not only can we declare that we are righteous, but we can also proclaim that we are holy and blameless—in Christ! But so few Christians—including many ministers—have grasped this truth.

A friend of mine recently served on his church's selection committee. In the process of interviewing candidates for a pastoral position, he asked each prospect, "Are you righteous?" My friend told me that the majority hemmed and hawed and responded by saying how imperfect they were. Finally one candidate responded with, "Do you mean positionally righteous in Christ? If so, the answer is *absolutely yes!*" He was hired.

Redemption: Purchased from Slavery

To many of us, *redemption* has become a generic phrase for

salvation. The biblical term, however, carries certain implications that unveil specific blessings we possess because of the cross.

The biblical meaning of the word *redeem* is "to deliver from slavery or from the captivity of an enemy by payment of a ransom."

The Bible states that because of our disobedience, we became slaves of sin, death, and Satan.[2] Jesus liberated us from that terrible triplet through His death. The New Testament states that "we have redemption through His blood," and that we "were not redeemed with perishable things like silver or gold...but with precious blood...the blood of Christ" (Eph. 1:7; 1 Pet. 1:18-19).

Other New Testament expressions, such as *ransom* and *deliverance*, are closely correlated with redemption. We'll look at them together because all of them denote a freedom from former bondage. (*Redeem* and *ransom* always imply a *price paid* for release, whereas *deliverance* does not.)

How exactly does Jesus' death free us?

Before we can answer that question, we must first learn something about Satan. It was Satan who enticed man to sin, who then gained "the power of death" as the book of Hebrews teaches us (see Heb. 2:14), and who now holds unregenerate humanity captive to do his will. Sin and death are both related to Satan to some degree because death came because of sin (Rom. 5:12), and Satan is the one who tempted Adam and Eve to sin in the first place.

The apostle John wrote that "the whole world lies in the power of the evil one" (1 Jn. 5:19), an obvious reference to Satan's dominion over unsaved people. Jesus referred to Satan as "the ruler of this world" at least three times (Jn. 12:31; 14:30; 16:11), and Paul once called him "the god of this world" (2 Cor. 4:4). A more accurate title would be "god of this *world's system.*"

Some have mistakenly thought that Satan has sovereign control over every earthly event, including governments, weather, volcanoes, and so on. The Bible, however, repeatedly affirms God is sovereign over the universe and our planet. Jesus referred to His Father as "Lord of heaven and earth" (Matt. 11:25). Satan is only ruling "the kingdom of darkness," of which all unsaved people are citizens. He is the "god of this world" because the people of this

---

[2] See Jn. 8:31-36; Rom. 6:6; Heb. 2:14-15; Eph. 2:1-3; 2 Tim. 2:24-26.

world are serving him whether they realize it or not.)

How did Satan obtain his position? We are not told in the Bible as much as, perhaps, we would like to know concerning Satan's past, but at least we know that Satan rebelled in heaven and was cast down to earth long ago (see Ezek. 28:12-19; Lk. 10:17-18). In the first pages of the Bible we find him tempting Eve in the garden of Eden, and when Eve, and then Adam, yielded to Satan's temptation, God's judgment fell upon them.

(Since they were free moral agents, God permitted Satan to tempt the first humans for the purpose of testing them. Had they not been offered a choice of obedience or disobedience, then they would have functioned as robots by virtue of their environment.)

God's Purpose for Satan

(Certainly the all-powerful God could have banished Satan—at his fall—to some other place in the universe, but He didn't. Satan was banished to earth for a purpose. His temptations would not only serve to test humans, but *if they yielded to his temptations, Satan would be given some degree of authority to administer the punishment for their transgressions, namely by inflicting them with death.)*

(God had told Adam that in the day he ate the forbidden fruit, he would die. Specifically, God was speaking of spiritual death because Adam and Eve did not die *physically* the day they ate the fruit—they died *spiritually*. At that time, Satan gained what the New Testament calls "the power of death" (Heb. 2:14). He was given permission, as an agent of God's wrath, to inflict sinners with spiritual and physical death.)

(*Spiritual death* is a term used to describe the spiritual disease that invades the spirits of humans who are in rebellion against God. It could be called the nature of sin, selfishness, or Satan, which infects the spirit of sinful individuals.)

We are told in the book of Hebrews that Jesus, "through death...render[ed] powerless him who had the power of death, that is, the devil; and might deliver those who through fear of death were subject to slavery all their lives" (Heb. 2:14b-15).

How did Jesus' death effect our release from Satan's captivity, sin, and death?

131

Stated simply, Jesus' death satisfied the claims of justice, making us no longer deserving of God's wrath. Thus sin, death, and Satan have no rightful hold over us. Satan can only afflict and hold in bondage those who are rightfully under God's condemnation. God has now "delivered us from the domain of darkness, and transferred us to the kingdom of His beloved Son" (Col. 1:13).

Now allow me to address the possible objections to what I've just stated. Some have surmised that somehow Satan got his authority illegally—that he is operating independently of God's purposes. But that is an impossibility.

God is the Creator and Lord over the universe, as Jesus Himself said,[3] and nothing can occur beyond His control. It was *God* who cast Satan from heaven after he rebelled, and obviously He permitted him access to the earth. Otherwise Satan wouldn't have been there to tempt the first humans.

If God cast Satan out of heaven, He could have easily kept him off the earth as well! Satan is operating within God's parameters. Satan would not have been able to afflict people with spiritual death unless God permitted it, which He obviously did.

Because Satan is bringing God's punishment upon evildoers, am I saying that God and Satan are co-workers?

No, God and Satan are not working together. God, who is all-knowing and all-wise, has obviously used Satan for His own purposes. There are very clear, specific examples in the Bible of God using Satan to deliver His judgments upon evildoers (see Judg. 9:22-24; 1 Sam. 16:14-23; Mal. 3:8-11; Matt. 18:21-35; 1 Cor. 5:1-5).

But God and Satan have different agendas. Satan is full of hatred. He wants people to sin. He wants them to suffer. He wants them to spend eternity in hell. God loves everyone. He doesn't want anyone to sin. He doesn't want anyone to suffer. He doesn't want anyone to spend eternity in hell.

But God *must* punish unrighteousness. The Bible makes that perfectly clear. The cross makes that perfectly clear. That's why God gave Satan the right to afflict sinners with "spiritual death," making it possible for Satan to hold them in captivity. This fact of

[3] See Matt. 11:25.

life is a foreshadowing to humanity of the ultimate wrath of God they will experience in hell. During this time of "earthly wrath," God is mercifully giving them time to repent and believe in Jesus and thus escape His full *eternal* wrath.

Some have swallowed a very simplistic theology of saying every "bad" thing that happens is from the devil, even things that the Bible often refers to as judgment from God. They unfortunately believe that God exercises no sovereign control over our earth, thus eliminating His holiness, wrath, and judgment with one fell swoop.

This whole theory comes very close to dualism, that is, the idea that there are two equal and opposing powers in the universe fighting each other. Satan is supposedly operating outside the realm of God's authority! That is absurd! God could instantly banish Satan to hell at this moment if He desired. Satan can do nothing other than what God permits. That is what the Bible teaches.[4] He is like a dog on a leash.

Breaking the Curse of Death

Obviously, the curse of Satan's dominion and death came as a result of God's judgment. God had forewarned Adam that he would die if he ate the forbidden fruit. Death came because of judgment, and the Bible says it was *Satan* who had the power of death. Only God could have given him that authority. T. J. Crawford correctly wrote:

> Our captivity to Satan is *judicial,* and is only a secondary consequence of our subjection to the wrath of God. Our enslaving foe is but, as it were, the subordinate instrument or executioner of God's righteous judgment. The grand requisite to our deliverance from his thraldom is, that the sovereign Judge should cancel or revoke our sentence.[5]

Through the curse of spiritual death and Satan's rule, God hopes that miserable sinners will come to their senses and believe the gospel. Contrariwise, Satan hopes they will continue rebelling

[4] For example, see Deut. 13:1-3; Job 1:9-12; Mal. 3:10-11; Lk. 22:31-32; 1 Cor. 10:13; 2 Thes. 2:8-12; Rev. 20:1-3, 7-10.

[5] Thomas J. Crawford, *The Doctrine of the Holy Scripture Respecting the Atonement,* p. 63.

against God, foolishly refusing Christ's pardon, so they will suffer everything they deserve in hell. But the "power of death" has been broken over those who believe in the Lord Jesus. We are not under Satan's dominion, and spiritual death has been removed from our spirits and replaced with God's divine life and nature. As Jesus promised, our spirits have been born again, and we have "passed out of death into life" (Jn. 5:24).

Moreover, we have no need to fear physical death because it promises better things for Christians. In addition, we can hope that we will be in that blessed group who will never face physical death—those who will be alive at Jesus' return. Then, as the Apostle Paul wrote, our bodies will experience redemption (see Rom. 8:23).

Can you see that the curse of spiritual death, the grip of sin, and the dominion of Satan were all a result of God's judgment upon sinners? Therefore, when atonement was made for sin through Jesus' death, those in Christ are no longer deserving of God's judgment.

Now notice how Paul, in his Colossian letter, couples the forgiveness of our sins through the cross with our deliverance from the devil through the cross:

> And when you were [spiritually] dead in your transgressions...He made you alive together with Him, having forgiven us all our transgressions, having cancelled out the certificate of debt consisting of decrees against us and which was hostile to us; and He has taken it out of the way, having nailed it to the cross. When He had disarmed the rulers and authorities, He made a public display of them, having triumphed over them through Him [some translations, rather then saying "through Him," make a direct reference to the cross, i.e. "on the cross"]" (Col. 2:13-15).

Paul is clearly writing metaphorically in this passage. Because of breaking God's law, we were like debtors, destined to spend an eternity in "debtor's prison," hell itself. But in Christ, our "certificate of debt" was nailed to the cross because Jesus bore our penalty, and across that certificate was stamped "paid in full."

On that same cross, Satan, who ruled us by the lesser evil spirits

134

referred to as "rulers and authorities," had his power broken by Christ. Paul metaphorically speaks of Christ's victory over Satan using the imagery of a practice in ancient warfare, when the returning, victorious army would parade their defeated captors in chains through the streets, publicly humiliating them.

Just as the cross was a revelation of God's righteousness, so, too, it demonstrated the end of Satan's rule over all those in Christ.

John Stott wrote concerning this passage:

> The bond [certificate of debt] he nailed to the cross; the powers he defeated by the cross....both happened together. Is not his payment of our debts the way in which Christ has overthrown the powers? By liberating us from these, he has liberated us from them.[6]

By God's righteous permission, Satan only has a right to dominate transgressors, and those who are in Christ are no longer transgressors but righteous new creations! That is how Jesus' death frees us from sin, Satan, and spiritual death. "If therefore the Son shall make you free, you shall be free indeed" (Jn. 8:36)!

Redeemed to be God's Children

However, we must not forget that, because we have been "purchased with His own blood," we are now considered "Christ's slaves"(Acts. 20:28b; 1 Cor. 7:22).

Two important scriptures that speak of redemption are found in Paul's letter to the Galatians:

> Christ *redeemed* us from the curse of the Law, having become a curse for us—for it is written, "Cursed is every one who hangs on a tree"—in order that in Christ Jesus the blessing of Abraham might come to the Gentiles, so that we might receive the promise of the Spirit through faith (Gal. 3:13-14; italics mine).

All of us were under God's curse because all of us have broken His laws. But Jesus has redeemed us from that curse by becoming cursed in our place on the cross. Because of it, even Gentiles can receive the promise that God made to Abraham, namely, God's

[6] John Stott, *The Cross of Christ*, pp. 234-244.

promise that *all* the families of the earth (not just the Jews) would be blessed through Abraham's seed, which Paul, a few verses later, explained was Christ.

In the fourth chapter of the same letter, Paul wrote:

> But when the fulness of the time came, God sent forth His Son, born of a woman, born under the Law, in order that He might *redeem* those who were under the Law, that we might receive the adoption as sons....Therefore you are no longer a slave, but a son; and if a son, then an heir through God (Gal. 4:4-5, 7; italics mine).

Redemption opens the door for our adoption into God's family; we relate to Him as His very own, full-grown sons. I can't think of a more blessed truth than that. We are God's own children, born of His Spirit. We are heirs of God!

Salvation: Deliverance from Sin and Sickness

The word *salvation* is an all-inclusive word that combines the ideas of propitiation, justification, reconciliation, redemption, as well as other New Testament expressions.

As it is used in the New Testament, the word *salvation* simply means deliverance, implying that we have been taken from an undesirable situation to a desirable one, which is certainly the case. We have been delivered from God's wrath (propitiation), from His condemnation (justification), from our mutual enmity (reconciliation), and from sin and the curse of the Law (redemption). When we survey the combined images these words depict, we can understand why the apostle described our deliverance as "so great a salvation" (Heb. 2:3).

Virtually all evangelicals agree as to the constituent benefits of salvation; however, there has always been some tension concerning exactly *when* one certain benefit is to be experienced. That benefit is physical healing.

All agree that when we experience what Paul calls "the redemption of our body," sickness will no longer be a part of human experience. Disease will have no dominion over our imperishable, glorified bodies. The question before us is, Have we any right to pray with faith, knowing that God desires our health in this present life?

From examining the New Testament, there is sufficient evidence to answer that question in the affirmative. The biblical usage of the word *salvation* is only one of many proofs that deliverance from sickness is not something we must wait until the next life to experience.

The Greek word used for *salvation* in the New Testament is *soteria*, derived from the word *sozo*, which is most often translated "saved." *Sozo* is also frequently translated "made well" when used in the context of cases of physical healing. It is clear from Jesus' own usage of the word that it not only implied forgiveness of sins but also healing of sickness.

In the *New American Standard* version of the New Testament, the word *sozo* is translated "made well" nine times. Three times it is translated "get well," and once it is translated "cured."[7] In every instance a physical healing was performed by Jesus. For example, when the woman with the issue of blood was healed, Matthew describes the incident by thrice using *sozo* within two verses:

> ...for she was saying to herself, "If I only touch His garment, I shall get well [sozo]." But Jesus turning and seeing her said, "Daughter, take courage; your faith has made you well [sozo]." And at once the woman was made well [sozo] (Matt. 9:21-22).

I encourage you to look up in a concordance the other references where *sozo* is used to speak of physical healing. The important point is that this same word is translated "saved" fifty times in the New Testament. It is obvious that the people of Jesus' day used *sozo* to mean deliverance from sin and deliverance from sickness and disease. (Often we find forgiveness of sins and deliverance from sickness coupled in the Bible.[8])

I realize that this in itself doesn't necessarily prove that God wants to heal everyone's sickness. However, if we can prove that sickness is a product of God's wrath or of Satan's evil doing (or both), then it is reasonable to believe that deliverance from

[7] "made well": Matt. 9:22,22; Mk. 5:34; 10:52; Lk. 8:36,48,50; 17:19; 18:42; "get well": Matt. 9:21; Mk. 5:23,28; "cured": Mk. 6:56

[8] i.e. Ps. 103:2-3; Matt. 9:2-8; Mk. 16:16-18; Jas. 5:15

sickness must be included in our salvation. We already know that on the cross Jesus delivered us from God's wrath and from Satan's dominion.

Who or What Causes Sickness?

In briefly searching the Scriptures, I've found at least twenty-seven clear references that prove sickness is often a manifestation of God's wrath against sin.[9] For example, a brief glance at the 28th chapter of Deuteronomy leaves no doubt that God uses sickness as a punishment for disobedience.

Furthermore, there are four clear references proving that Satan afflicts people with sickness and disease (often as the agent of God's wrath or discipline).[10]

Therefore, if Jesus has saved us from God's wrath and from Satan's dominion, then why would we ever think that God wants us to remain sick? I realize some have reasoned that God wants us to remain sick to teach us some lesson or develop character in us, but you won't find such logic in the Bible. Jesus never told anyone who came to Him for healing, "I want you to remain sick so you'll learn a lesson and develop character." No, Jesus healed *all* who came to Him seeking physical healing.

Yes, God may permit sickness to attack a Christian in order to bring him to repentance (see 1 Cor. 11:30-32), but it is not God's will for him to remain sick. If he repents, he can be healed.

And certainly the Bible teaches that we can grow during trials and adversity, but sickness is in a different category. The Apostle James wrote:

> Is anyone among you *suffering*? Let him pray....Is anyone among you *sick*? Let him call for the elders of the church, and let them pray over him, anointing him with oil in the name of the Lord; and the prayer offered in faith will restore the one who is sick, and the Lord will raise him up, and if he has

[9] See Gen. 20:17-18; Ex. 9:8-16; 23:25; Num. 12:1-15; 16:46-50; Deut. 7:15; 28:1-63; 1 Sam. 5:9; 2 Sam. 12:15; 1 Kin. 8:37; 2 Chron. 21:12-18; 30:18-20; Ps. 38:3; 106:15; 107:17-22; Is. 10:16; 33:24; Jer. 16:4; Mic. 6:13; Matt. 9:2; 13:15; Jn. 5:14; 12:40; Acts 28:27; 1 Cor. 11:30; Jas. 5:15; Rev. 2:22.

[10] Job 2:6-7; Lk. 13:10-16; Acts 10:38; 1 Cor. 5:5

committed sins, they will be forgiven him (Jas. 5:13-15; italics mine).

Notice that James had different instructions for one who is sick compared to one who is suffering in other ways.

And also notice that James did not qualify his healing promise as only for certain individuals. It is for *anyone* who is sick. The Lord *will* raise him up in response to the prayer of faith. And if sin is the reason he is sick, forgiveness is promised as well.

Of course, it is only the prayer of faith that brings healing. Prayers of hope don't bring spiritual salvation and neither do they bring physical salvation. Therefore, the one praying must be convinced it is God's will for him to be healed, just as he had to be convinced that it was God's will for him to have his sins forgiven in order to be saved.

Healing in the Atonement

Has physical healing been provided for us in Christ's atonement? Absolutely yes. It amazes me that many say healing has not been provided for us by Christ's death, yet at the same time they affirm that one day we will all live without sickness or disease in heaven. How has that future deliverance from sickness been provided? Those same people who deny that healing is provided in the atonement will have to say that our *future* health has been provided by the atonement! We're not going to be sick in heaven because Jesus died for our sins. Jesus, on the cross, merited the redemption of our bodies. Thus, those who say that healing is not provided for us in the atonement are contradicting themselves.

The question then is, Should we expect to experience now, or only later, the healing Jesus has provided for us? Of course, some want to push it off to the future. It is certainly true that there are benefits of salvation that we won't experience until the future, such as life in heaven, seeing Jesus face to face, and so on. But there are benefits we can experience right now, such as forgiveness, adoption, rebirth, and the baptism in the Holy Spirit. Into which category does healing fall, present or future?

The obvious answer is that healing is something provided for us *now*. Under the Old Covenant, physical healing was often provided for the people by means of an atoning sacrifice, and it was provided, not for some future day, but for the present (see Lev. 14:1-32; Num. 16:46-50; 21:5-9 with Jn. 3:14-15).

Of course, the Old Testament sacrifices only prefigured Christ's atonement, which provides healing, not just for the future, but also in the present.

Jesus never said to anyone who came to Him requesting healing, "No, you can't be healed now, but you'll be healthy in heaven."

During His earthly ministry, Jesus forgave sins *and* healed the sick. He also sent His disciples out to heal the sick (see Matt. 10:8; Lk. 10:9) and said one of the signs that should follow believers is that they will lay hands upon the sick and they will recover (see Mk. 16:17-18).

In the early church, many people were healed as recorded in the book of Acts. In addition, the healing promise found in the book of James reflects the apostles' teachings on this matter.

Obviously, healing is a present benefit.

But some will object, saying, "Just because God healed others doesn't guarantee He'll heal me."

They don't realize that they've just assaulted the love and justice of God. God loves all equally. He is, as the Bible says, "no respecter of persons." If God will forgive the sins of *one* who repents and believes, He'll forgive the sins of *all* who repent and believe. If God healed *one* in response to his faith, God will heal *all* who pray to Him believing.

The Healing Gospel

The "healing gospel" is not some new idea that originated with the Pentecostals early in this century. In fact, it predates even the New Testament by centuries. Isaiah wrote of the healing benefit of Christ's atonement at least 700 years before any of the New Testament was written. His great 53rd chapter plainly tells us that healing would belong to us because of Jesus' sacrifice:

> Surely our griefs He Himself bore [the margin indicates that *griefs* could also be translated "sickness," and anyone who studies the Hebrew will agree that "sickness" is a much more

accurate translation[11]], and our sorrows He carried [the margin indicates that sorrows could be (and should be) translated "pains"[12]]. Yet we ourselves esteemed Him stricken, smitten of God and afflicted. But He was pierced through for our transgressions, He was crushed for our iniquities; the chastening for our well-being fell upon Him, and by His scourging we are healed (Is. 53:4-5).

There is absolutely no doubt that this passage refers to physical healing. Matthew confirmed this when he stated that the healing of many people at Peter's house was a fulfillment of what Isaiah wrote:

And He touched her [Peter's mother-in-law's] hand, and the fever left her; and she arose, and began to wait on Him. And when evening had come, they brought to Him many who were demon-possessed; and He cast out the spirits with a word, and healed all who were ill in order that what was spoken through Isaiah the prophet might be fulfilled, saying, "He Himself took our infirmities, and carried away our diseases" (Matt. 8:15-17).

Sadly, some have argued that the healings Jesus performed during His earthly ministry *completely* fulfilled Isaiah's prophecy. Yet I ask, Why don't they also say Jesus completely fulfilled the portions of Isaiah's 53rd chapter promising forgiveness of sins when He forgave people during His earthly ministry?

Obviously, if we maintain that we can be forgiven because Jesus bore our sins according to Isaiah 53, then we can also maintain that we can be healed because Jesus bore our sickness according to the same chapter.

Healing cannot be classified as only a future heavenly benefit of salvation because it has been experienced by so many here on earth. We don't find Jesus passing out crowns, giving people glorified bodies, or letting them walk on golden streets during His

---

[11] The word translated "griefs" is the Hebrew word *kholee*, which is translated "sicknesses" in Deut. 7:15; 28:61; 1 Kin. 17:17; 2 Kin. 1:2; 8:8; 2 Chron. 16:12; 21:15.

[12] The word translated "sorrows" is the Hebrew word *makob*. It is translated "pain" in Job 14:22; 33:19 and Jer 51:8.

earthly ministry, but we constantly find Him healing sick bodies. Healing is a benefit for the present age.

That is why the crippled man in Acts 14 was healed while listening to Paul preach the gospel. It is quite obvious that the *salvation* (sozo) of which Paul preached included deliverance from sickness as well as from sin:

> ...and there they [Paul and Barnabas] continued to preach *the gospel*. And at Lystra there was sitting a certain man, without strength in his feet, lame from his mother's womb, who had never walked. This man was listening to Paul as he spoke, who, when he had fixed his gaze upon him, and had seen that he had faith to be made well, said with a loud voice, "Stand upright on your feet." And he leaped up and began to walk (Acts 14:7-10; italics mine).

How did this man acquire faith to be healed? The Bible says faith comes from hearing the word of Christ (Rom. 10:17). His faith came from hearing Paul preach the gospel, and so Paul's message *must* have included physical healing.

What would happen if that same gospel were preached today? We don't have to speculate because some *are* preaching that gospel today, including myself. When it is preached, people are delivered from sin *and* sickness. I know from personal experience, however, that people in non-western nations are more likely to have faith for healing because they have not been brain-washed (or better, "brain-dirtied") against divine healing by the usual unscriptural theological arguments. But anyone, east or west, can receive what Jesus purchased for him. It is only a matter of faith.

Some object to the healing portion of salvation by claiming that if it were true, then everyone who is saved would also automatically be healed. But this is not true. The constituent benefits of salvation must be individually appropriated. A person can be saved but remain sick just as he can be saved and remain guilty or filled with fear of Satan. The Bible tells us that although Israel possessed most of the promised land, they still left unconquered areas that belonged to them by God's promise (see Jug. 1:27 - 2:2). So too, healing is for every Christian to individually possess.

How to Get Well

If you are sick, how can you get well?

First of all, make certain that your sickness has not been permitted by God because of your disobedience (see 1 Cor. 11:28-32). Don't try to drag something up to condemn yourself, but if you know you've been disobedient, then confess your sins. God promises to forgive you, so there will be no hindrance to your healing (see Jas. 5:14-15; 1 Jn. 1:9). Look particularly in your heart for unforgiveness because unforgiveness is listed in Scripture as something that can open the door to God's discipline (see Matt. 18:34-35).

Second, make certain you are not violating any of the natural laws of health. If you are not taking proper care of God's temple (your body), you can't expect Him to heal it. Your body must have enough sleep, and it must have the sufficient vitamins and minerals to work properly. Many Christians aren't sick so much as they are malnourished or even poisoned. We have learned that humanism dominates American cuisine, and we suffer for it, thinking we can improve upon God-given foods. You wouldn't pour paint into your car's gas tank, and neither should you put something into your body that isn't designed by the One who created your body.

Third, make sure you *truly* believe that it is God's will for you to be healed. If you're not convinced, your doubts will stop your healing. Spend time reading, meditating upon, and speaking the healing promises in the Bible. It might take some time for your faith to grow.

Perhaps you have been "brain-dirtied" by unbelieving theological reasoning. I recommend that you read either *Christ the Healer,* by F.F. Bosworth (published by Revell) or *Healing the Sick,* by T.L. Osborn, (published by Harrison House). Both books are excellent faith builders for anyone seeking healing, and the authors answer the common faith-destroying arguments against divine healing.

Fourth, pray in faith, believing that God has heard and answered your prayer according to His promises and Mark 11:24. If you believe, then begin thanking God for healing you. He will see to it that His promise comes to pass in your body!

Your testimony can be just like David's:

Bless the Lord, O my soul; and all that is within me, bless His holy name. Bless the Lord O my soul, and forget *none* of His benefits; who pardons all your iniquities; *who heals all your diseases* (Ps. 103:1-3; italics mine).

So Great a Salvation

The study of the achievement of the cross is so broad that this chapter could easily grow into volumes. In fact, a pastor could spend his entire ministry expounding upon this one subject.

I encourage you to invest your time studying such subjects as adoption, sanctification, heirship, regeneration, imputation, identification, election, citizenship and glorification. They're all part of our amazing salvation. Thank God for our full salvation provided for us by our wonderful Savior when He suffered for us on the cross, bearing our penalty!

TEN

The Cross in Practice

I sincerely hope that your heart has been captured by the cross of Jesus Christ. Once we understand the significance of Jesus' death, our lives can never be the same. Like a new pair of eyes to one legally blind, the cross enables us for the first time to see things clearly, both far and near. The cross reinterprets every situation; it colors every view; it rights every wrong perspective. By it we interpret history and predict the future. By the cross we see every person in a new light. By it our motivations are brought into focus and our hearts are laid bare. By the cross the eyes of our understanding are opened.

In this final chapter, I want to share five specific ways that the cross alters our former perceptions. To what degree have our hearts been captured by the cross? Let us examine our lives as we survey the following five indicators.

1. If the cross has truly captured our hearts, we live for a new purpose.

In fact, Jesus and His cross become the *only* things worth living for. If God became a man and suffered and died to offer forgiveness to people who are otherwise destined to spend eternity suffering in hell, then those who believe it must live to spread that message.

The saddest thing is not that people refuse to believe in Jesus, but rather that some people have never yet been given an opportunity to make a choice. What could possibly be more important than making certain everyone hears "the word of the cross," the gospel of Jesus Christ? Nothing. *Absolutely nothing.*

Those who have been captured by the cross live for one purpose. They may not be pastors or evangelists. They may be flight attendants, construction workers, homemakers, or business executives. Whatever their occupation they are missionaries to their world and seek opportunities to witness of God's saving grace through Christ.

As we meditate upon the message and revelation of that cross, our supreme prayer request is that the world hear the gospel. Our aspiration becomes to be used of God as He sees fit and take the gospel to those who have not yet heard it. We live for Christ's cause.

Today many Christians are caught up in other worthy causes, but none compares to the worthiness of spreading the gospel. Lately, it seems that political involvement is being presented as the Christian's most sacred duty. But is it? The good that results from political action is immensely inferior to that of preaching the gospel. If all Christians would be as devoted to spreading the gospel as some are in their political involvement, there would be much less need for political activism.

The best way to improve society is by means of the gospel. People who are born again don't abort their babies; they don't patronize pornographic theaters; they don't abuse their children; they don't sell drugs.

Imagine for a moment a person sitting in a crowded football stadium. Somehow he learns that a small atomic bomb buried in the middle of the football field is going to be detonated in thirty minutes.

He thinks to himself, "I must tell these people to evacuate the stadium." So he dashes from his seat in search of the broadcasting booth to announce the peril of the situation and instruct the spectators to evacuate.

In his search, he accidentally ends up in a public restroom and sees profanity scribbled all over the walls. "Oh!" he says to himself, "I would hate for some child to come in here and see this." So he diligently begins to scrub down the walls of the restroom for the next thirty minutes to remove the profanity.

No one would argue that the man was involved in a worthy cause as he worked to clean up the restroom. But while he worked with zeal, a stadium full of people was blasted into eternity.

This exemplifies the activities of many Christians today. They are doing good things, but while they work, people are slipping into an eternal hell as the seconds tick off.

To make matters worse, the world often perceives Christians as people who are trying to make the world conform to their morality. The media presents us as religious fanatics whose sole message is one of political conservatism. Unbelievers reject what they *think* is our message, never hearing the message we are supposed to convey to them.

Why are Christians against abortion, gambling, alcohol, and pornography? Because they have been born again and given a new nature. When they became children of God, their perspective of everything changed. If we want others to see things as we do, then let us use the same means that changed our perspectives. Let us proclaim the gospel! The gospel is the solution to society's ills.

Am I saying that Christians shouldn't be involved in the political process? No. In a democracy, Christians have an obligation to be involved. But may our political involvement never supersede our gospel involvement. Let us work to change unsaved people's hearts, and then their minds will be changed also.

2. When our hearts are captured by the cross, our perception of the world changes.

The Apostle Paul wrote:

> But may it never be that I should boast, except in the cross of our Lord Jesus Christ, *through which the world has been crucified to me, and I to the world* (Gal. 6:14; italics mine).

When Paul understood what happened on the cross, he became a different man—a man of another world. All his former ambitions died. His love of this life and his selfish pursuits died. He viewed the world as something that needed to be redeemed—a world that would one day perish, a world of which he was no longer a part.

Material things become unimportant to those whose eyes are fixed upon the cross. Next to it, diamonds lose their sparkle and gold's luster fades. Knowing that the things of this world are destined to burn one day, the one who has been captured by the cross invests in things eternal. He would rather win someone to Christ than own a Rolls Royce. And if owning a certain object might possibly hinder someone from coming to Christ, he never buys it.

He knows that more possessions cannot bring true joy and fulfillment. By supporting missionaries, by sharing with those less fortunate, by printing gospel tracts, the believer sees his money as simply a tool for bringing the gospel to more people. If he desires to make a lot of money, it is not to buy bigger and better toys. It is because he wants to invest more in the kingdom of God. He loves to give.

Many have speculated as to why the early Christians in Jerusalem so generously sold homes, lands, and possessions to lay the proceeds at the apostles' feet. Some have theorized that they were specifically led by the Holy Spirit to do so because He knew their city would be destroyed by the Roman Legions. But that is unlikely since they were selling their possessions more than thirty-five years before the Roman siege.

The answer is simply that the early Christians had been captured by the cross. Material things no longer held their hearts. Christ did. They valued their possessions only as potential tools to win people to Christ.

The one who has been captured by the cross sees himself, not as a citizen of this earth, but as a citizen of heaven where his Savior dwells. The believer is only a sojourner here, and his treasure is being laid up in heaven. Everything of this world is viewed as only temporal and, therefore, of no real value. All personal accomplishments before his salvation are regarded as worthless.

The believer finds it hard to imagine Jesus, looking down from His throne on Judgment Day and saying to the retired executive: "Way to go! I'm impressed! You worked hard at your job and got to the top! You were able to buy anything you wanted!" As for that day, the one who values the cross knows his heavenly reward depends on what he has done to advance God's kingdom on earth.

3. When our hearts are captured by the cross, our perspective of the people of this world changes.

We no longer categorize people as rich, poor, black, white, American, or Russian. It no longer makes a difference to us. People are either saved or unsaved; they are either sinners or saints. When our hearts are captured by the cross, the question that comes to our mind when we first meet someone is, "I wonder if he's saved?"

Because of the cross, we know God loves everyone immensely, regardless of their sinfulness. We also know that a way has been provided for them to escape the wrath of God. Now we see people through the eyes of the One who died for them.

Paul wrote it this way:

> For the love of Christ controls us, having concluded this, that one died for all, therefore all died; and He died for all, that they who live should no longer live for themselves, but for Him who died and rose again on their behalf. *Therefore from now on we recognize no man according to the flesh*...(2 Cor. 5:14-16a; italics mine).

Now we recognize people *spiritually*, either as born again or as dead in their trespasses and sins. And now the love of Christ, which He demonstrated so marvelously on the cross, controls us.

We must love our enemies. How can we hate those whom God loves? We who have been shown so much mercy are obligated to show mercy to everyone.

When we are reviled, we do not revile in return, but pity and pray for our persecutors. We know if they don't repent, they'll suffer even more in hell for having reviled us. God loves those who harm us and wants them to accept their pardon. He loved them so much He died for them.

We know it was not the nails that held Jesus to the cross, but His love for humanity.

4. When our hearts are captured by the cross, our perception of the people of God's kingdom changes.

Before I was saved, I used to make fun of "Jesus freaks." Who would have believed that one day I would be one! If I could find any of the "Jesus freaks" I used to mock, I'd hug them as my brothers and sisters.

Our fellow-believers are our brothers and sisters, members of God's family. We would rather spend time with them than with many of our own natural relatives (if they are still unsaved). We love our brothers and sisters in Christ and are careful to avoid doing anything that could cause them to stumble. The Apostle Paul wrote:

> For if because of food your brother is hurt, you are no longer walking according to love. Do not destroy with your food him *for whom Christ died* (Rom. 14:15; italics mine).

> For through your knowledge he who is weak is ruined, the brother *for whose sake Christ died*. And thus, by sinning against the brethren and wounding their conscience when it is weak, you sin against Christ. Therefore, if food causes my brother to stumble, I will never eat meat again, that I might not cause my brother to stumble (1 Cor. 8:11-13; italics mine).

Jesus said,

> "This is My commandment, that you love one another, just as I have loved you. Greater love has no one than this, that one lay down his life for his friends" (Jn. 15:12-13).

We are commanded to love our brothers, following the example Jesus set before us when He laid down His life for us. Who are we to decide whether or not to love one of God's own children? John wrote in his first epistle that it is impossible to hate God's children and love God at the same time (see 1 Jn. 4:20).

All the fighting and bickering in the body of Christ indicates that our hearts have not been captured by the cross. Our pet doctrines often divide us because we're all following a few teachers whom we think are infallible. But the cross puts an end to all that.

The Corinthian Christians were being divided by their varying preferences for certain teachers, and Paul addressed their carnality by bringing them back to the cross:

> Now I mean this, that each one of you is saying, "I am of Paul," and "I of Apollos," and "I of Cephas," and "I of Christ." Has Christ been divided? *Paul was not crucified for you, was he?* Or were you baptized in the name of Paul? (1 Cor. 1:12-13; italics mine).

When we are captivated by the One who was crucified for us, we cannot be enamored by any favorite teachers. Wouldn't it be wonderful to open one of our modern Christian magazines and see, instead of endless promotions of personalities, praise for the One who died for us! Sometimes I wonder if it's "ministry-anity" instead of Christianity" that we espouse.

When our hearts have been captured by the cross, denominational walls crumble. Now that we love all those for whom Christ died, we can no longer restrict our fellowship to our own exclusive church or group. We may not always agree on certain doctrines, but all of us can join hands around the cross.

To the Methodists, Presbyterians, Pentecostals, Baptists, and Charismatics who have been captured by the cross, our labels elicit more shame than pride, indicting us for our division and lack of love. We would prefer to be known only as Christians.

5. When our hearts are captured by the cross, our perspective of ourselves changes.

First, the cross brings an end to pride.

As we see Jesus hanging there, suffering for our sins, we begin to realize how debased we are. How foolish we were to think that we could save ourselves or merit our salvation by our good works. It was our sin that condemned Him. Our selfishness nailed Him to that cross, and the awfulness of our sin is revealed there.

Once we've accepted our pardon and received His righteousness, we realize that everything we are and will be is because of Him. Since our gifts and talents originate from His grace, they should only glorify Him. All boasting ceases. The Apostle Paul

151

wrote, "But may it never be that I should boast, except in the cross of our Lord Jesus..." (Gal. 6:14a).

The cross is our only boast, for without it we have nothing and are nothing.

Second, the cross brings an end to unforgiveness.

How can we, once we realize the price that was paid so we could be forgiven, hold unforgiveness against those who have wronged us? In the light of the cross, unforgiveness is exposed as self-righteousness. By harboring a grudge, we are in effect saying, "You have wronged someone who has never wronged another. You are guilty of something of which I'm not."

You'll recall Jesus' parable of the unforgiving servant who was forgiven an astronomical debt by his master but who was unwilling to forgive his fellow-servant a small amount by comparison. The message of this parable is obvious: the servant had no right to be merciless when he himself had experienced so much mercy. The Bible says his master was "moved with anger" and "handed him over to the torturers until he should repay all that was owed him" (Matt. 18:34).

Jesus then promised: "So shall My heavenly Father also do to you, if each of you does not forgive his brother from your heart" (Matt. 18:35).

This means that if we persist in harboring a grudge, God will permit Satan to afflict us until we repent. In effect God says, "So you want to treat others with fairness rather than with mercy? You want them to receive everything they deserve? Then I'll treat you with less mercy and more fairness. I'll let you have a taste of what you deserve."

Paul wrote that we are obligated to forgive because we have been forgiven through Christ's cross:

> Let all bitterness and wrath and anger and clamor and slander be put away from you, along with all malice. And be kind to one another, tender-hearted, forgiving each other, just as God in Christ also has forgiven you (Eph. 4:32).

Third, the cross brings an end to selfishness.

One cannot understand and believe what happened on the cross and continue to live purely for his own selfish pursuits. There is no way a person could rightfully react to the cross by saying, "Yes, I believe that the Son of God died for me. Now I'm going to live for what I can get."

The supreme example of love, demonstrated by Jesus' agony while He was suspended between heaven and earth, moves us to lay down our lives for those for whom He died. The author of our salvation was selflessness personified. From the cross He calls us to deny ourselves, inspiring us by His great example. Paul wrote:

> Do nothing from selfishness or empty conceit, but with humility of mind let each of you regard one another as more important than himself....Have this attitude in yourselves which was also in Christ Jesus, who....humbled Himself by becoming obedient to the point of death, even death on a cross (Phil. 2:3-8).

> ...and walk in love, just as Christ also loved you, and gave Himself up for us, an offering and a sacrifice to God as a fragrant aroma (Eph. 5:2).

To what degree have our hearts been captured by the cross? The answer is revealed by the love we spread.

Carrying Our Cross

It has often been debated as to what Jesus meant when He said, "If anyone wishes to come after Me, let him deny himself, and take up his cross daily, and follow Me" (Lk. 9:23).

Some say that God gives each of us some burden to carry. I've met people who claim their sickness is their cross; others say their job or their spouse is their cross. But I don't think so.

The cross of which Jesus spoke is something we *voluntarily* take up, not something God, or the devil, or circumstances force upon us. In order to take up our cross, Jesus said we must deny ourselves. Our cross is something we must carry daily if we are to follow Jesus.

Some have pointed out that Jesus was speaking here not of *His* cross but *our* cross, thereby concluding they must be two different crosses. But the New Testament teaches that Christ's cross *is* our cross. We have been crucified *with* Him. When one learns that

Christ's cross is his cross, he has heard the gospel. And when we take up our cross daily, it is Christ's cross that we carry.

What did Jesus mean? He, of course, knew that His cross should be the center of all true theology, the hub of all heavenly revelation, the heart of the message that God wants conveyed to all humanity. He knew it should be the standard by which everything is measured, the key to all of God's blessings, and the banner that marks the true church. He knew the gospel would be known as "the word of the cross."

Jesus meant that His cross, our cross, should dominate our daily lives. Through it we should view every person, situation, circumstance, and opportunity. By it we should judge ourselves and show others mercy. It represents the message we are called to proclaim and the life we are called to live. *True disciples have had their hearts captured by the cross.*

Last Words

There can be only one reason for an anemic church—because she is malnourished. To be strong the church must continually feed upon the Word of God, nourishing herself with a *balanced* diet. I fear, however, that much of what the church has been consuming is junk food. We must return the cross to the place it deserves—as the main course of every meal.

Respected pastor, Jack Hayford, recently wrote:

> I believe that the charismatic movement must chart a fresh course to the central point of Christian truth: the cross of Jesus. The remedy for any imbalance is precisely there, where those two crossbars remind us of the need to balance heaven's requirements (vertical) with human need (horizontal).[1]

Only the cross can restore balance. It is the foundational truth of the Bible. We know that if a building's foundation is faulty, then the whole structure will collapse. Jesus, His person and His work, must be returned as the chief cornerstone. Only then can the church can be built properly, "a spiritual house for a holy priesthood, to offer up spiritual sacrifices acceptable to God through Jesus Christ" (1 Pet. 2:5).

[1] Jack Hayford, *Charisma*, Sept. 1990, p. 74.

Pastor Hayford went on to say:

> One recent study of the content of most charismatic worship music indicated that both Christ's cross and His blood are scarcely mentioned. Does this drift from the biblical and historical center of Christian faith signal a warning? I think so. It's hard to synchronize this tendency with the theme song of heaven, both now and eternally; "To Him [the Lamb] who loved us and washed us from our sins in His own blood" (Rev. 1:5; see also 5:9).

> The cross must command center stage in our lives, ever and always; and as participants in this revival, let us be certain it does in the charismatic movement as well. The cross is the fountainhead of all God's wisdom, as well as the source of all His power (1 Cor 1:18-25; 2:1-4).

> Let's start singing again, "Jesus, keep me near the cross." *Humility* is assured there, which will keep arrogance and pride from gaining ascendance. *Holiness* is assured there, which will keep presumption and ungodliness at bay. *Love* abounds there, which will help us to hear each other and to keep the teachable heart of a child. Finally, the *power* is there—for the fountainhead of all Christ's glory-workings toward humankind was opened there. We must keep that fountainhead as our foundation—resting all our revelations and blessings on the footings that Calvary provides.[2]

E.W. Moore, a clergyman in the church of England in the early 1900's, witnessed first-hand the historic Welsh revival. Upon observation of the amazing ministry of Evan Roberts, the primary human agent in that revival, Moore passionately wrote,

> He has had a vision of Calvary....He has seen "One hanging on a tree, in agonies and blood," and the sight has enthralled him....What we need is a fresh vision of the Cross. And may that mighty, all-embracing love of His be no longer a fitful, wavering influence in our lives, but the ruling passion of our souls.[3]

[2] Jack Hayford, *Charisma*, Sept. 1990, p. 76.

[3] E.W. Moore, *The Story of the Welsh Revival*, p. 82.

This book is only a primer on the greatest subject ever studied—the cross of Christ. My hope is that it will inspire ministers and lay-people alike to reevaluate everything that is done under the banner of Christianity. Let us return to the foundation of our faith. Let us once more place Christ's cross where it belongs: in the center of everything we say and do. If we will, sermons will change, churches will change, lives will change, cities will change, and for multitudes, eternity will change.

Bibliography

Crawford, Thomas J. *The Doctrine of Holy Scripture Respecting the Atonement* (1871). Grand Rapids: Baker Book House, 1954.

Dale, R.W. *The Atonement.* London: Congregational Union, 1899.

Denny, James. *The Death of Christ.* New York: George H. Doran Co., 1902.

Finney, Charles G. *Revivals of Religion* (1835). Cambridge, MA: Harvard University Press, 1960.

Hayford, Jack. "A Remedy for Imbalance", *Charisma*, September, 1990, Vol. 16, No. 2.

Henry, Matthew. *Commentary on the Whole Bible* (1710?). Grand Rapids: Zondervan, 1961.

Kittel, G. ed. *Theological Dictionary of the New Testament*, Vol. 1. Grand Rapids: Eerdmans, 1964.

Lloyde-Jones, D. Martyn. *The Cross.* Westchester, IL: Crossway, 1986.

McDowell, Josh. *Evidence that Demands a Verdict.* San Bernardino, CA: Campus Crusade, 1972.

Moore, E.W. (contributing author). *The Story of the Welsh Revival.* New York: Fleming H. Revell Company, 1905.

Morris, Leon. *The Apostolic Preaching of the Cross.* Grand Rapids: Eerdmans, 1965.

_____. *The Atonement:* Its meaning and significance. Downers Grove, IL: InterVarsity, 1983.

_____. *The Cross of Jesus.* Grand Rapids: Eerdmans, 1989.

Packer, J.I. *Knowing God.* Downers Grove, IL: InterVarsity, 1973.

Pelikan, Jaroslav ed. *Luther's Works,* Vol. 26. (1535). St. Louis: Concordia Publishing House, 1963.

Rudolph, L.C. *Francis Asbury.* Nashville: Abingdon Press, 1966.

Smeaton, George. *The Doctrine of the Atonement According to the Apostles* (1870). Peabody, MA: Hendrickson, 1988.

Spurgeon, C.H. *Lectures to My Students* (1875). Lynchburg, Virginia: The Old-Time Gospel Hour, no date.

Stalker, James. *The Trial and Death of Jesus Christ.* Grand Rapids: Zondervan, 1983.

Stott, John R.W. *The Cross of Christ.* Downers Grove, IL: InterVarsity, 1986.

Tozer, A.W. *The Knowledge of the Holy.* New York: Harper and Row, 1961.

Scripture Index

161

About ETHNOS
Correspondence Bible School

Do you desire to accelerate your spiritual growth? Do you feel called to minister to others? Are you hungry for in-depth teaching that is practical, biblical, and anointed by the Holy Spirit?

Then you'll want to write and ask for information about *ETHNOS Correspondence Bible School.* You can receive cassette tape recordings of live classes taught at *ETHNOS School of the Bible* by Rev. David Kirkwood. Take as many or as few classes as you like. Work at your own pace. If you desire, you can take classes for credit and work toward a diploma.

Numerous courses are offered for your spiritual enrichment, such as *Scriptural Spiritual Warfare, The Book of Philippians, The Bible on Healing, Building Your Self-Esteem Through God's Word, The Book of Daniel, The Cross of Christ, The Book of James, Living in the Unselfish Realm, God's Economics, The Gospel of Luke, The Holy Spirit and His Gifts,* and *The Christian Family.* Each course contains eight life-changing, power-packed teachings. Tuition costs are very affordable.

For more information, write *ETHNOS Correspondence Bible School*, P.O. Box 0446, Library, PA 15129. Your life can be transformed by God's Word and the Holy Spirit!

Also by David Kirkwood...

Your Best Year Yet is a daily devotional-commentary that will help you read through the entire Bible in one year. This easy-to-read devotional follows the reading plan of the *One Year Bible*®, and contains inspirational reflections, historical background notes, and life-changing applications for each day's reading from the Old and New Testaments. Discover fresh insights from God's Word to help make this ...*Your Best Year Yet!* Available at your local Christian bookstore or by using the order form below. (ISBN 0-88419-274-1, 480 pages, Trade paper, $15.95)

Lead your loved ones to Christ by giving them *Forgive Me For Waiting so Long to Tell You This*. In this easy-to-understand book, David Kirkwood shares the gospel in a logical, biblical, and *very* convincing manner. Your friends and loved ones will be respectfully confronted with the amazing love of God and the claims of Christ. They'll understand the significance of Jesus' death. And they may very well receive Jesus as their Savior and Lord. (ISBN 0-9629625-0-3, 132 pages, Trade paper, $6.95)

You can also order additional copies of *Christ's Incredible Cross* by using the order form below, or save postage and handling costs and order from your local Christian bookstore.

Book Title	No. of copies	Price	Extended Price
Forgive Me For Waiting so Long to Tell You This		$6.95	
Your Best Year Yet		$15.95	
Christ's Incredible Cross		$7.95	
Add $2.00 shipping and handling per book		$2.00	
Total Amount Enclosed			

Send order form and payment to: ETHNOS Press, P.O. Box 0446, Library, PA 15129

When your write, ask for information about **ETHNOS Correspondence Bible School**, and teaching tapes by David Kirkwood.